Maintaining Family Ties

Inclusive Practice in Foster Care

Sally E. Palmer

REUNIFICATION

FAMILY PRESERVATION PROGRAM
921 BEASLEY ST.
SUITE 103
LEXINGTON, KY 40509

Child Welfare League of America • Washington, DC

CHILD WELFARE LEAGUE OF AMERICA, INC.
440 First Street, NW, Suite 310, Washington, DC 20001-2085

CURRENT PRINTING (last digit)
10 9 8 7 6 5 4 3 2 1

Cover design by Paul Butler
Text design by Eve Malakoff-Klein

Printed in the United States of America

ISBN # 0–87868–599–5

This book is dedicated to my sister, Nancy Maki,
who gave generously of her interest and support, and to
the many children whose feelings may be overlooked
because they lack power in the foster care system.

Contents

Acknowledgments

Many people helped to create this book. Dean Ralph Garber collaborated in my application for research funds, George Thomson supported the project for funding by the Ontario Ministry of Community and Social Services, and Roma Scott managed the project. Winifred Koneri, Catholic Children's Aid Society of Metropolitan Toronto, and Arne Petersen, London Family and Children's Services, facilitated access to the agencies. Excellent research assistance was given by Connie Murray, Lynn Macintyre, and Fiona Johnson. James Gladstone gave selflessly of his precious research time to study and advise on the first draft, and Carol Speirs provided support as a child welfare expert with similar ideals. Eileen Pasztor offered advice and encouragement, and Carl Schoenberg provided direction and painstaking accuracy in his editing. My daughter Ellen, my husband Earl, and my son Bruce all provided encouragement over the years of research and writing.

Introduction

The Importance of
Maintaining Family Ties

Family attachments are central to the psychological development of children.* Theories of separation [Bowlby 1973] and self-concept formation [Rosenberg 1979] lead us to expect that children who are uprooted from their own families are likely to experience object loss and identity confusion. As a result, it is accepted in the child welfare field that children in care need help in dealing with separation, particularly in maintaining ties with their families.* Accepted theory, however, is not being implemented in practice.

Recent trends in child welfare have strengthened the arguments for including children's families in planning for their future. These trends include efforts to normalize the children's environment, plan for permanency, and prepare older children for living independently.

The principle of normalizing the child's environment underlies, for example, the trend to keep even very disturbed children in their own communities, in surroundings that approximate family life. The trend to normalization has led agencies to develop treatment foster homes for very difficult children who might otherwise be sent to specialized facilities in other commu-

---

* The term *children* is used generically and is intended to include adolescents when the use of both terms would be cumbersome. When the focus is on children age 13 and over, they are generally termed *adolescents* or *youths*.

**In accord with the principle of keeping children's families involved in their lives, the term *family* is reserved for the biological family, and the term *foster carer* is used instead of *foster parent*.

nities. As a consequence, the use of specialized foster care has expanded [Hudson & Galaway 1989]: specialized family foster carers tend to receive more training and consultation than traditional foster carers; they are also reimbursed for their time and knowledge, rather than just for expenses. Compared to traditional foster carers, specialists are treated more as colleagues in their agencies: besides handling the ongoing difficulties characteristic of disturbed children and adolescents, they have tended to broaden their therapeutic work to include the child's family. The trend to normalization has brought into question the traditional model of workers intervening between families and foster carers [Forsyth 1989].

Permanency planning refers to the goal of providing stability for children, either through reunion with their families, adoption, or placement in a long-term substitute home [Maluccio et al. 1986]. This philosophy has directed attention to the desirability of preventing placement by preserving children's families and avoiding the instability that often characterizes out-of-home care. Research has shown that entry of a child into care may be only the beginning of a series of moves from one unsuccessful placement to another [Lawder et al. 1986; Berridge & Cleaver 1987]. If preserving the family fails and the child is placed, attention to the family should continue. First, children's best chance for permanency is still with their families [Fanshel 1982]; empirical studies have shown that the likelihood of reunion is increased when regular parental contact is sustained [Fanshel & Shinn 1978; Palmer 1983]. Second, continuity of family ties is essential to children's well-being [Colon 1978]; in cases where children's safety and security needs preclude reunion, "preservation of family should be recognized as preservation of ties and attachments, rather than preservation of actual living arrangements" [Kufeldt 1990]. Furthermore, children's stability in placement may depend upon their resolving their feelings about being separated from their families [Tiddy 1986].

Finally, greater attention is being given to the preparation of older children when they leave care to live independently [Mech 1988]. Young people who have not found a permanent home, either with their families or in a long-term placement, will eventually move to independent living because of their age. It often becomes apparent at this point that agency intervention, although it may have been necessary, has contributed to a vacuum in the youth's life. Many youths are found to be without any meaningful family ties: they may have moved from one home to another, or have simply failed to form close ties even after a long-term placement [Raychaba 1988]. Such situations point to the breach that occurs between children and their families when the children enter agency care. Placement is often the agency's option of last resort for children who are neglected or abused or adolescents whose families want them "out." Too little fore-thought is given to the future circumstances of youths whose family ties may be lost by the time they leave care. The likelihood of this breach is heightened now that an increasing number of adolescents is entering care. Adolescents are even less likely than younger children to form strong relationships with their caregivers that will carry them through to adult life. Consequently, placement puts adolescents at risk of losing their family connections, and of being unable to replace these connections with any other meaningful relationships.

These trends in child welfare have given new relevance to the maintenance of links between children in care and their families. Little research has focused on workers' interventions with children's families, however. Many articles and books offer advice on the topic, but few offer empirical data on what workers actually say and do with children. One study observed that workers' "cognitive understanding [of children's needs] was not necessarily translated into practice" [Kufeldt 1990].

Over the years, the author has explored informally and (as a supervisor) formally the attitudes and knowledge of child placement workers concerning interventions to help children with separation reactions. It has proved difficult to elicit any concrete information about what workers actually do. As a supervisor, the author found that workers were reluctant to discuss their own roles; when pressed, they would describe the children's verbal and behavioral expressions of feeling, with little mention of how they themselves responded. An examination of case records of 200 children in the long-term care of two Canadian Children's Aid Societies yielded similar results: workers made little mention of their own interventions to help children with their feelings [Palmer 1976]. The silence on this topic suggests either that the workers did not try to help children with their separation feelings, or that the workers were unable (or perhaps unwilling) to describe their interventions. Additional empirical studies are needed to find out how workers are actually handling this aspect of placement.

The Study Setting

The empirical study presented in this book is based on the reports of 36 social workers in two child protection agencies about the experiences of children on their caseloads. The study examines the children's behavior and expressed feelings related to separation from their families, as well as the responses of their workers, foster carers, and placement agencies. To help readers judge the extent to which the findings may be generalized to their own circumstances, the context in which this practice took place is described here in detail.

The children reported on were in the care of two child protection agencies in the province of Ontario, Canada. In Ontario, the responsibility for child protection is carried by 54 Children's Aid Societies (CASs), which are mandated by provincial legislation to provide child protective services, in a manner similar to that of public child protection agencies in the United States. The

54 CASs cover the entire province, which has a population of almost 2.5 million children. Three of Ontario's largest cities have large Roman Catholic populations, so each of these cities has two CASs—one nonsectarian and one under Roman Catholic auspices. In four communities, special agencies have been set up by Native Indian bands,* or groups of bands, to provide child protection services for their own people.

At any one time, there are about 10,000 children in Ontario CAS care [OACAS 1992]. Some minority groups tend to be overrepresented. For the two agencies where the study took place, the racial distribution of children in care (N = 403) was: Asian 12%, Aboriginal 10%, and Black 4%. Corresponding representation of these minorities in the Ontario population (N = 9.98 million) was Asian 8%, Aboriginal 0.7%, and Black 2.5% [Statistics Canada 1993]. Similar overrepresentation of minority groups in care is found in many parts of the United States, where the most vulnerable families tend to be African American, Hispanic, and Native American [Stevenson et al. 1992].

Several influences require or encourage CASs to maintain links between families and their children in foster care: legislation, government monitoring, voluntary collaboration, and workers' education, training, and experience.

Legislation

The 1984 Ontario Child and Family Services Act (CFSA) mandates that CASs provide child protective services, including the placement of children in substitute care. This legislation supports the maintenance of family ties in its stated principles, sets forth stipulations about parental access, requires a Plan of Care, provides

---

* Bands in Canada are similar to tribes in the U.S., except that *band* refers to people living in one location. Members of a particular Indian Nation, such as the Mohawks or Senecas, might live in a number of different communities, with each community being designated as a band.

for review of placements by an independent committee, and places a two-year limit on children staying in agency care without a permanent transfer of custody away from their parents.*

A major principle underlying CFSA is that of supporting families, rather than rescuing children from them. One of CFSA's primary purposes is "to recognize that while parents often need help in caring for their children, that help should give support to the autonomy and integrity of the family unit and, wherever possible, be provided on the basis of mutual consent" [Ontario 1984: 8]. Thus, agencies are expected to work with families, as long as children are not in imminent danger, and provide counseling, instrumental assistance, or family preservation services to keep the family intact. If these services are not sufficient to ensure a minimum standard of child care, a CAS may take over care and control of the children, either through parental agreement or court order. About 15% of children in care are there by voluntary parental agreement; the remainder are there by court order [OACAS 1992]. In keeping with the principle of supporting families, care and control of a child is granted to a CAS only when it can prove to the court's satisfaction that it has done everything possible to keep a family together.

When judges award care and control of children to a CAS, they are required by CFSA to make an order concerning parental access to the children. If there is reason to fear that a child might be harmed during visits, the order may require the agency to supervise parental contact. Parental access tends to be denied only in extreme cases of child abuse.

Under CFSA, when a CAS requests a court order regarding a child, it must also present a Plan of Care, developed in collaboration with the biological parents as well as the children (if they

---

* When children are in temporary agency care, they are called *Society wards* and the CAS is awarded "care and control" over them. This contrasts an order for permanent care, in which children are called *Crown wards*, and the CAS is awarded "custody," that is, the CAS becomes the official parent who is legally responsible for the child.

are old enough). The plan includes such items as the expected duration of agency care, the conditions under which the children will be returned to their parents, and the frequency of family contact. For children who are in care by parental consent, rather than court order, CFSA's regulations require that the CAS develop a similar plan for every child within 30 days of admission to care, and revise those plans every 90 days thereafter.

CFSA requires that each jurisdiction covered by a CAS establish a Residential Placement Advisory Committee (RPAC). These committees are independent of the CASs and comprise a service provider, a government representative, and a local citizen. Their main purpose is to protect the rights of children in nonfamily placements, in particular residences with a minimum of ten beds (defined as *institutions*). Each committee reviews the placement history of the children under its jurisdiction and provides the children with an opportunity to make known their concerns and wishes, which may relate to family contact and/or possible reunion. For children in institutions, an RPAC hearing must be held within 45 days of the placement and every nine months thereafter. Children 12 and over who object to their placements, whether in institutions or not, must be given a hearing within 14 days of their placement and once every nine months thereafter. Moreover, most RPACs will invite parents to the hearing or, failing this, elicit their views by letter or telephone contact. The RPACs ensure that an agency's placement practices are open to the scrutiny of independent county representatives.

Since 1954, child welfare legislation in Ontario has placed a limit of two years on maintaining children in care without terminating the rights of their parents. At the end of two years, the court cannot make a further order for temporary care and control by the CAS. If the CAS wants to retain the child in care, it must apply for an order of Crown wardship, a term that refers to the provincial government's power as the Queen's representative. An order for Crown wardship places the child in the permanent custody of the Ontario government (represented by the

CAS), and makes the government into a "parent," that is, it entitles the government to exercise all the rights and duties of a parent. In applying for Crown wardship, the CAS has the burden of demonstrating to the court that it has made every possible effort to maintain family involvement and work toward the child's return home, or that family involvement would be damaging to the child.

In child welfare hearings, parents who want to regain care and control of their children are usually represented by lawyers, who cross-examine workers about their efforts in behalf of the family. This practice further opens CAS placement practices to public scrutiny, making the agency publicly accountable for its ongoing work with families. Even when Crown wardship is granted, if the CAS has no immediate prospect of placing the child for adoption, the court usually grants parents continuing access. The CAS must return to court to have the right to access terminated if and when it does find an adoptive home.

The legislation under which CASs operate provides a structure that strongly encourages the maintenance of family ties. The intent of this structure is viewed in Ontario as similar to that of legislation on permanency planning in the United States, particularly the Adoption Assistance and Child Welfare Act of 1980 (Public Law 96–272). The U.S. legislation promotes maintenance of family ties by requiring child welfare agencies to make "reasonable efforts" to enable children to remain safely at home before the court will support placement in out-of-home care, and to move children out of custodial foster care and back to their families, to adoptive placements, or to long-term foster homes, giving priority to family reunion. The U.S. legislation also provides for citizen review, not unlike that of Ontario's RPACs.

Government Monitoring

The Ontario government is responsible for financing the work of the CASs and for monitoring their adherence to legislative requirements. For these purposes, the government has developed standards and guidelines for foster care, in accordance with the principles and requirements of CFSA. These standards and guidelines give priority to family reunification as the best alternative for children in care, and encourage agencies to keep families involved with their children in care.

It should not be assumed that all of the above structures are consistently applied. The Ontario government personnel who monitor CAS adherence to legislation tend to have unrealistically high caseloads: for example, one staff member may be responsible for two large urban agencies, which between them employ approximately 500 social workers. Moreover, the government rarely sanctions agencies that fail to meet its standards: the only meaningful recourse is to revoke the agency's charter, but this has been done only about once in a decade. Generally, the government's monitoring role is limited by insufficient resources and by a lack of alternatives to CAS services.

Voluntary Collaboration

All Ontario CASs belong to an umbrella organization, the Ontario Association of Children's Aid Societies (OACAS), which upholds standards of practice by publishing a monthly journal and holding an annual conference.* The conference is an opportunity for child welfare professionals (frontline workers, supervisors, and managers) to share information about policies, programs, and methods of intervention. At these conferences, presentations are usually made concerning work with the families of children in care and helping children with the sequelae of separation.

Workers' Education, Training, and Experience

Most Ontario child welfare workers—particularly those working in urban centers—have a university degree in social work. In 1993, the educational qualifications of frontline social workers

---

* OACAS developed and began implementing standards for CAS practice in pilot agencies in 1992, but they were not in place at the time of the study.

(N = 1,888) in Ontario's CASs were: M.S.W. 23%; B.S.W. 44%; B.A. 16%; Community College Certificate (two years postsecondary education) 11%; and other 6% [OACAS 1993]. The workers in this study (N = 36) had slightly higher educational backgrounds: M.S.W. 22%; B.S.W. 55%; B.A. 12%; Community College 2%; and other 9%. A social work degree does not ensure that workers have had specific education in child welfare, but only that they have been educated in generic social work knowledge and skills, including child development and interviewing, which are part of the curricula required by the Canadian Association of Schools of Social Work, the accrediting body for social work degree programs. Consequently, workers with a social work degree would have been exposed to developmental theory, including attachment and identity formation, and to the importance of eliciting and responding to children's feelings in crisis situations, such as separation from their families. It is difficult to generalize about practice from the urban agencies in this study to those in rural and remote parts of Ontario, however, where workers are less likely to have a social work degree.

As for in-service training, most Ontario CAS workers are given three weeks of government training in basic child welfare knowledge and skills, including theory and practice principles related to separation of children from their families. Sixty-two percent of the 36 foster care workers in this study reported having four hours or more of training in separation. In addition, the project integrated with the study provided 20 hours of training in understanding and handling separation with children. Finally, the 36 workers in the study had a fair level of experience, as 74% had been in CAS work for two or more years.

The Ontario child welfare system is quite highly structured to ensure attention to children's family ties, although it has some large loopholes. The workers implementing the system have a fair level of training, education, and experience. The 36 workers who provided the information on which the study is based were selected at random* to receive special training in separation theory and its application to placement practice. Working within these structures, the agencies and workers responsible for foster care in Ontario are exposed to many influences that encourage them to be inclusive of biological families.

Using this Book

This book is intended mainly for child welfare practitioners and students. It sets out the theory related to parent-child separation and applies it to foster care, and reviews the literature showing how this theory has been implemented or ignored in placement practice. Through its analysis of audiotaped sessions between workers and their supervisors, it examines the practice of 36 child welfare workers in dealing with children's reactions to separation and thus fills a gap in practice research.

Chapter One presents theories of separation and self-concept relevant to children in care. Chapter Two reviews research knowledge from empirical studies and practice experience. Chapters Three, Four, and Five describe and discuss the qualitative findings from workers' discussions in supervision, including children's reactions to separation; workers' interventions; and agency influences on the handling of separation. Chapter Six draws conclusions and makes recommendations.

Appendices A to D provide details of the format and content of the in-service training program on separation and inclusive practice that was given to the workers at the project's beginning.

References

Berridge, D., & Cleaver, H. (1987). *Foster home breakdown*. Oxford, England: Basil Blackwell.

---

* Six teams of six workers each were randomly picked from a pool of 12 teams as part of the experimental design.

Bowlby, J. (1973). *Attachment and loss: Vol. 2. Separation.* New York: Basic Books.

Colon, F. (1978). Family ties and child placement. *Family Process, 17,* 289–312.

Fanshel, D. (1982). *On the road to permanency: An expanded data base for service to children in foster care.* New York: Child Welfare League of America.

Fanshel, D., & Shinn, E.B. (1978). *Children in foster care: A longitudinal investigation.* New York: Columbia University Press, 1978.

Forsyth, P.W. (1989). Family preservation in foster care: Fit or fiction? In J. Hudson & B. Galaway (Eds.) *Specialist foster family care: A normalizing experience* (pp. 63–73). New York: The Haworth Press.

Hudson, J., & Galaway, B. (Eds.). (1989). *Specialist foster family care: A normalizing experience.* New York: The Haworth Press.

Kufeldt, K.A. (1990). Developing a model for involving natural parents. In B. Galaway, D. Maglajlic, J. Hudson, P. Harmon, & J. McLagan (Eds.), *International perspectives on specialist foster family care* (pp. 111–123). St. Paul, MN: Human Service Associates.

Lawder, E.A., Poulin, J.E., & Andrews, R.G. (1986). A study of 185 children 5 years after placement. *Child Welfare, 65,* 241–251.

Maluccio, A., Fein, E., & Olmstead, K. (1986). *Permanency planning for children and youth.* London: Tavistock Press.

Mech, E. (1988). Preparing foster adolescents for self-support: A new challenge for child welfare services. *Child Welfare, 67,* 487–495.

Ontario Association of Children's Aid Societies. (1992). *Services survey 1992.* Toronto, ON: Author.

Ontario Association of Children's Aid Societies. (1993). *Human resources survey 1993.* Toronto, ON: Author.

Ontario Child and Family Services Act 1984.

Palmer, S.E. (1976). *Children in long-term care: Their experiences and progress* (research report). London, ON: Family and Children's Services, 1976.

Palmer, S.E. (1983). *The effects of training child welfare workers in separation* (doctoral thesis, University of Toronto).

Raychaba, B. (1988). *To be on our own with no direction from home: A report on the special needs of youth leaving the care of the child welfare system*. Ottawa, ON: Youth in Care Network.

Rosenberg, M. (1979). *Conceiving the self*. New York: Basic Books.

Statistics Canada. (1993). *Ethnic origin. 1991 Census of Canada, Catalogue 93–315*. Ottawa, ON: Industry, Science, and Technology Canada.

Stevenson, K.M., Cheung, Kam-Fong M., & Leung, P. (1992). A new approach to training child protective services workers for ethnically sensitive practice. *Child Welfare, 71*, 291–305.

Tiddy, S.G. (1986). Creative cooperation: Involving biological parents in long-term foster care. *Child Welfare, 65*, 53–62.

Chapter One
Attachment, Separation, and Identity Theory and Their Implications for Foster Placement

To understand the effects of removing children from their families and placing them in foster care, it is necessary to examine theories of attachment, separation, and identity formation. These concepts originated in traditional psychoanalytic theory, and have been gradually modified and refined within a framework generally known as developmental theory.* In discussing attachment and separation, reference is mainly to younger children; the discussion of self-concept and identity formation is focused primarily on adolescents.

Attachment

The process of attachment is believed to be a basic adaptive response by infants to their need for protection, comparable in strength of motivation to feeding and mating behaviors [Bowlby 1982]. Accordingly, the attachment formed by infants to their primary caregiver is of overwhelming importance to their psychological security. The caregiver becomes the infant's first love object and the medium through which the infant will develop the capacity for other emotional relationships.

---

* Most of the theory in this chapter is supported by references to the literature; occasionally the author makes inferences from existing theory, and from her own experiences with foster placement as a worker, supervisor, and staff trainer.

Ideally, infants form a secure attachment to a primary caregiver that allows them to seek independence gradually and eventually develop a sense of identity as an autonomous, valuable individual. In somewhat less secure environments, infants develop anxious attachments. When environments are extremely unreliable or unresponsive, infants are unable to form basic trusting relationships and lack the foundation for building a sense of self.

Secure Attachment

The development of secure attachment is thought to take place as follows. As postulated by Mahler et al. [1975], infants younger than six months of age have a subjective sense of being merged with their caregivers in a symbiotic relationship. Behavior indicating attachment is typically observed in young children between six and 36 months of age. Children of this age tend to promote proximity and contact with their mothers by "seeking, approaching, grasping, clinging and following" [Lieberman 1987: 112]. Gradually, children move beyond this stage to a perception of the caregiver as a need-satisfying "object"; by 30 to 36 months of age, children have usually established a sense of psychological separateness [Mahler et al. 1975].

Psychological separateness is thought to be achieved through the development of *libidinal object constancy* [Fraiberg 1969], defined as "that state of object relations in which the child has the capability to retain the memory of and emotional tie to parents...and to feel their nurturing, guiding presence even when they are absent" [Solnit 1982: 202]. This capability allows the developing child to tolerate situations of increasing independence, a necessary process for building a separate identity. As children develop a sense of their own autonomy, they are increasingly able to relate to others as separate individuals with needs of their own. This ability lays the foundation for reciprocal relationships, in which children look beyond their own needs to those of others.

The kind of infant-parent relationship associated with secure attachment has been observed by researchers who studied infants left by their mothers in a "strange situation" [Ainsworth et al. 1978]. The strange situation was a laboratory experiment in which one-year-old children were exposed to three-minute episodes of increasing stress in an unfamiliar environment. The infant was first in a strange playroom with her mother,* then with a stranger, then alone. The mothers of securely attached infants tended to respond sensitively to their infants' expressed needs, allowing their infants to use them as a secure base from which to explore new situations. If the mother left the room, her infant might protest or search for her; but was quickly reassured by her return and immediately sought close body contact.

Anxious Attachment

In the above experiment, infants were assessed as "anxiously attached" when they ignored their mothers on reunion, had temper tantrums, or made only intermittent efforts to seek closeness to their mothers [Ainsworth et al. 1978]. The definition of anxious attachment is generally used for infants when the mother's presence does not support exploration or reduce distress following separation [Farber & Egeland 1987].

Young children who are maltreated by their parents seem especially prone to developing anxious attachment. A study of 18-month-old children whose parents had physically abused, neglected, or been psychologically unavailable to them, found that they were anxiously attached to their parents [Egeland & Sroufe 1981]. Although abused children may show relief when placed with better caregivers, "they may nonetheless feel the loss deeply and show separation anxiety" [Provence 1987: 97].

---

* When pronouns indicating gender are used, a balance will be maintained by alternating between the masculine and feminine forms.

"Unintegrated" Children

Children who fail to make any meaningful attachment to a caregiver are defined as "unintegrated" [Balbernie 1974]. These children lack an adequate "primary experience," that is, the experience of reliable nurturing from a mother figure. Lacking such nurturing, they have not been able to internalize the sense of well-being that enables other infants to cope with separation. Without this capacity, unintegrated children act out their anxieties, cannot identify with the feelings of others, do not show guilt, and fail to value themselves.

Early research showed a tendency to nonintegration in children who had been institutionalized because their mothers were in jail. Spitz [1945] compared children from a foundling home, who were cared for by various staff members after weaning at four months, with those from a residential nursery, whose mothers were incarcerated but regularly spent time with them. Because the foundling home staff worked in shifts, Spitz hypothesized that the children would have difficulty in attaching to a primary caregiver; according to attachment theory, this could be expected to retard their development. The hypothesis was supported: the foundling home children had a better average developmental score at admission than those in the nursery; but this position was reversed after the age of four months, the age when the foundling home infants were weaned and their "modest human contacts stopped" [Spitz 1945]. An even greater discrepancy related to mother contact was shown by mortality rates in the two homes: 37% of 91 infants in the foundling home died within two years of the first study; none of the 122 infants in the nursery died over a three and one-half year period [Spitz & Wolf 1946].

Further support of attachment theory comes from a follow-up study of young children who had been institutionalized in infancy. As young children, they showed superficial emotional responses and poor capacity for social discrimination [Goldfarb

1945]. At follow-up when these children were adolescents, they had difficulty in forming relationships, and showed a lack of guilt over antisocial behavior [Goldfarb 1955]. A different study, following up children at age eight, confirmed that early institutionalization had an adverse effect on development [Tizard & Hodges 1978].

In summary, theory and empirical research indicate that children's psychological development depends profoundly on their forming a secure attachment with their primary caregiver. Even children whose relationships are insecure, and who are anxious in their attachments, have a stronger base for development than children whose primary relationships were interrupted after being established.

Separation

Attachment theory provides a basis for, and is supported by, theories concerning separation. The term *separation* is sometimes used to refer to the normal child-initiated differentiation from a primary attachment figure. In this discussion, however, separation refers to an externally initiated event that forces children to live apart from their primary objects of attachment. Separation is not always forced, as some adolescents seek protection or relief from their families. Even for them, however, separation may become an issue when their initial feelings of relief begin to give way to an awareness of loss.

As discussed above, the separation of children from their primary attachment figures arouses feelings of anxiety and loss. If the separation is prolonged, these feelings may create psychological disorganization and depression. To cope with their reactions, children invoke ego defenses. The following discussion deals with children's feelings and defenses, variables that may be expected to influence their responses, and implications for their psychosocial development.

Anxiety and Sense of Loss

A corollary of attachment theory is that children will experience anxiety and loss when separated from their primary caregiver. Empirical studies have shown that children react to separation with anxiety and attempts to regain the lost person. The studies involved separations in everyday situations, in placement (including hospitalization), and in laboratory demonstrations.

Bowlby [1973] studied children younger than age four in everyday separation experiences, such as venturing from their mothers' side to explore a park. He found they commonly showed anxiety on becoming aware of their distance from their mothers. He also identified a number of environmental conditions to which young children reacted with fear, at least occasionally; those most germane to foster placement were exposure to strange situations (people, objects, and surroundings) and being left alone. When two or more of these conditions were presented simultaneously, children's fear tended to increase.

Children age 12 to 36 months were observed when separated from their mothers for hospitalization or residential placement [Robertson & Bowlby 1952]. They protested their mothers' absence verbally and loudly, they searched for them, and they made persistent efforts to bring them back, using behavior that would normally achieve contact. Separation anxiety was also shown in a study by Ainsworth and colleagues of one-year-olds who were introduced to "strange situations" in the laboratory: the infants cried and searched for their mothers [Ainsworth et al. 1978].

Slightly different results were found in a study of children age 18 to 30 months who were fostered by the researchers while their mothers were hospitalized to give birth [Robertson & Robertson 1971]. Elaborate arrangements were made to cause minimal disruption in the children's lives, yet they showed mild anxiety during the first few days, evidenced by their unfocused activity and frequent outbursts of unprovoked laughter. Subsequently, their distress increased: their laughter and activity were largely superseded by frustration and tears. This study group differed from those in other studies in that these children made little effort to get their mothers back; they were probably well prepared for the separation by discussion in the home about the new baby's arrival. Although anxiety and distress seem to be inevitable, it may be possible to preempt the child's efforts to achieve reunion in situations where they have no chance of success.

Despair and Depression

When children's protests do not achieve reunion with a lost parent, they have been observed to enter a stage of despair, followed by depression [Robertson & Bowlby 1952]. Despair is a transitional phase: deserted children continue to express strong feelings, as in the protest phase, but their focus moves from seeking the parent's return to expressing their pain at the loss. The ability to feel and express despair is a sign of emotional health in children, as it reflects strong attachment and the ability to tolerate pain without repressing it prematurely.

Children move to the depression phase when they become hopeless about achieving reunion. In this stage, they withdraw, appearing to lose interest in the environment or in other caregivers. An extreme example of this was found in the study of mothers in prison [Spitz & Wolf 1946] whose infants were weaned at four months and placed in a residential nursery. When the infants were studied, at ages six to 12 months, they showed all the symptoms of depression. Their outward appearance was one of complete withdrawal, rejection, and turning away from the environment; they could be engaged in play only when an adult spent up to an hour to achieve such engagement.

Findings from animal research have also been identified as relevant to children in foster care, that is, mammals tend to respond to overwhelming stress by learned helplessness—an alternating pattern of hyperarousal and numbing [Fine 1989]. Young animals traumatized by complete maternal and social deprivation were found to respond to stress by flight, fight, and freeze reactions rather than adaptation [Van der Kolk 1987]. This explanation goes beyond the simple designation of children in care as depressed; it may help to explain why some children seem to function fairly normally, but are limited in expressing their feelings and forming close relationships.

Defenses against Painful Feelings

As mentioned above, emotionally healthy children allow themselves to experience some pain at the loss of a parent, but use ego defenses to deal with the pain. Most commonly, children use denial to fend off initial anxiety; later, if they undergo the expected transition to depression, they are likely to use detachment.

Children in denial tend to behave as though the separation was not happening or was not important. Their use of denial seems to correlate with the degree of trauma involved in the separation. In the laboratory experiments, children seemed to react as soon as they were aware of the mother's absence [Ainsworth et al. 1978]. In Robertson and Robertson's [1971] study of "minimal disruption" out-of-home care, the children's unfocused laughter and activity suggest denial, in view of their eventual expression of painful feelings. Because it is normal for children to protest separation, children who show little reaction are probably denying its impact on them.

Detachment was found in placed or hospitalized children following the stages of overt protest, despair, and depression [Robertson & Bowlby 1952, cited by Lieberman 1987]. The children showed renewed interest in their environment and seemed to have distanced themselves emotionally from their mothers. This detachment is a means of dealing with depression, that is, children reduce their conscious sadness by repressing their yearning to have their mothers back.* The detachment is also a means for children to protect themselves against pain associated with future separations. If the mother returns during this phase to visit or reclaim her child, the child continues at first to repress any positive feelings. She appears not to recognize and even turns away from her mother. This is not a simple forgetting, as the child will concurrently give recognition to other relatives who have been absent for a similar time [Robertson & Bowlby 1952, cited by Lieberman 1987]. Similar detached behavior in young children is often reported by mothers who have returned home from holidays: they describe their children as being "angry at me" or "paying me back." Detachment as a defense is gradually given up if the mother remains; the child alternates between clinging to and rejecting the mother for a time, then returns to normal [Robertson & Robertson 1971].

If the mother fails to visit regularly or does not return, the child will probably incorporate detachment as part of his developing personality. He has, in effect, aborted the normal process by which people mourn the loss of a loved one. Psychologically healthy adults can tolerate the pain of detaching themselves slowly, and begin to reintegrate their lives without denying the importance of their attachment and loss. Because young children feel overwhelmed by their loss, however, they may force themselves prematurely into the detachment phase. As a result, "The intense yearnings coupled with anger are not given free expression, are suppressed, and continue to exert a hidden negative effect on the child's unfolding personality" [Lieberman 1987: 118].

Adults, including professionals, may collude in cutting off the child's grieving process. There is little social reinforcement for young children to express their feelings about the loss of a

---

* The term *mother* is used for ease of expression, but the theory could as well be applied to a father who was the child's primary caregiver.

parent, whether through death, marital separation, or foster placement of the child. Professionals working with adults in mourning tend to encourage active grieving, with the goal of catharsis and reintegration of the personality; they are less likely to do this with children, probably because it is so painful to watch a grieving child. Adults typically tend to protect children from the immense grief they are expected to feel by trying to distract them or assuming that their parent(s) can be replaced. Thus, children are supported in using defenses such as denial and detachment to deal with separation. This may have a permanent stunting effect on their emotional development.

Conditions Influencing Effects of Separation

Rutter [1972] questioned Bowlby's theory of maternal deprivation as inevitably damaging to children's mental health. He contended that it was possible for children, under favorable circumstances, to survive separation from their parents with relatively good mental health. The important variables were thought to be the characteristics of the individual child and the quality of care received before the separation [Rutter 1979; Tizard & Hodges 1978]. These variables have not received much empirical attention, with the exception of the age of the child at separation.

Age. As children mature, different forms of separation cause them to be anxious. Infants in their first six months react to strangeness in the general environment, not to the absence of a particular loved person. Infants under six months of age who were moved from foster to adoptive homes showed only temporary distress [Yarrow 1964].

After six months of age, infants begin to fear the loss of a particular loved person; the most vulnerable period is between seven months and three years of age. Marvin [1977] found that most children become distressed, even in brief laboratory-type separations, with slight variations in their reactions according to

Intervening Variables. Children's anxiety about their mother's absence can be mitigated by supportive conditions [Lieberman 1987]. These conditions include

> empathetic acknowledgment of the child's feelings as understandable and legitimate, reassurance that the mother loves him and will return, and availability of a stable substitute caregiver who serves as a secondary attachment figure and as an external support and reliable extension of the child. [Lieberman 1987: 130]

Separation can also be mediated by the child's use of "transitional objects," that is, by allowing the child to have a familiar blanket, stuffed animal, or toy as a parent substitute, thereby ameliorating the pain of aloneness [Winnicott 1971]. In the study of minimal disruption foster care, the researchers used transitional objects (the child's own bed, blankets, and toys; the mother's picture) to minimize loss [Robertson & Robertson 1971]. This could account for the child's ability to cope with the first few days of separation and the ease of reconciliation on the mother's return.

Strangeness for children can be minimized by the presence of a familiar person and place [Bowlby 1973]. Robertson and Robertson [1971] operationalized this concept by using a familiar caregiver, preplacement visits, and daily visiting by the child's father. The children showed far less distress during and after the separation than the placed and hospitalized children observed earlier by Robertson and Bowlby [1952]. These findings are complemented by the laboratory finding that children could tolerate a potentially frightening situation when an adult, especially a parent, was present to give support [Ainsworth et al. 1978].

Implications for Child Development

Mahler [1963] and Erikson [1963] view separation of the child from the primary caregiver as an interruption to development. As explicated by Mahler [1963], separation-individuation is a long-term process that unfolds as the child is developmentally ready and desirous of functioning independently. Any prolonged separation from a primary love object is an arbitrary interruption of this gradual process; it forces children to make adaptations that violate normal developmental processes.

Erikson's widely accepted model of developmental stages from infancy to adult autonomy [1963] provides a useful framework for understanding the possible effects of separation. Erikson postulates that children at different ages have to complete certain life tasks and resolve certain conflicts. The child's relationship with the primary caregiver is central to these tasks and conflicts, especially in the early years; thus, separation of children from their parents will impede or complicate their development.

In Erikson's model, the major psychological task for children in their first two years of life is the development of trust in their parents. Children who have been able to trust their parents, but who subsequently lose them, will have some basis for establishing trust with subsequent parent figures. When children have been unable to rely on their biological parents, however, the lack of a base of trust will undermine their future relationships. Younger children tend to blame themselves for difficulties with parents; as they become older, they begin to differentiate between their parents' responsibilities and their own. If the parent-child relationship is interrupted in the early years, the child is more likely to internalize a sense of self-blame.

At age two, the child's primary task is to begin establishing an independent identity. Children who have reached this stage of testing out their separateness from their parents need a stable relationship in order to successfully complete the stage. Separation of the child from her parents at a time when she is beginning to assert her autonomy interrupts the process of individuation. Further, the child may believe that her resistance to parental authority has caused the separation and feel guilty.

To a great extent, children develop their sexual identities by modelling themselves on their same-sex parent. Thus, it is important for children to have a consistent, positive model for this process. Interruption of family relationships leaves children to find other models, which may create confusion if placement is with a family from a different class or culture.

During the preteen years, the achievement of social competence with peers becomes paramount and family relationships tend to be taken for granted. Children need to be reassured that their relationships with parents are stable so that they can invest their energy outside the home. If their attention has to be concentrated on family crises or making adjustments to moves, their social and intellectual learning will be hampered.

For adolescents, the major task is to achieve psychological independence from the family, that is, to develop an autonomous identity. As with the two-year-old child, the assertion of independence needs to take place within a secure relationship; physical separation from the family makes the task immensely complicated. In particular, physical separation interrupts the normal process of conflict and resolution in daily living that characterizes the relationships of most adolescents with their parents. Adolescents need to feel they can express difference and still be accepted by their families; if they are living apart because of family problems, they will feel uncertain about their status as accepted family members.

In addition to the potential consequences to the child of separation from the parents at each developmental stage, it is relevant that Erikson's stages are interdependent, in that each successive stage depends upon the successful completion of tasks from the previous stage. Accordingly, the earlier the child's separation from the primary caregiver, the more complex will be the child's task of progressing through subsequent developmental stages.

Two empirical examples show the retarding effect of separation on infant development. In the research of Spitz and Wolf [1946] in the residential nursery, institutionalized infants became withdrawn after losing contact with their mothers; moreover, when their mothers returned, there was a dramatic improvement in their functioning. All their earlier symptoms were reversed and their tested "developmental quotients" increased [p. 330].

In the laboratory studies of one-year-old infants by Ainsworth and colleagues, the children's exploration of the environment decreased in their mothers' absence [Ainsworth et al. 1978]. The children were helped somewhat by the presence of a supportive stranger, but they still functioned at a lower level than when their mothers were present.

Identity

The foregoing theory and research suggests that a sudden, enforced separation from parents is likely to have a profound effect on a child's development. This section discusses the formation of identity, including its dimensions of belonging, autonomy, self-esteem, and stability of self-concept, and the potential effects of separation on identity formation. Emphasis is placed on adolescents, as identity formation is crucial for them, just as attachment is paramount in the earlier years.

Definition

Erikson defines *identity* as the accrued experience of the ego's ability to integrate inner feelings, aptitudes, and social roles [1963: 261]. He stresses the importance of identity as a prerequisite for intimacy in relationships: only those who have a secure identity can risk the self-abandonment of committing themselves to another that is required for intimacy [Erikson 1963: 263–264].

Rosenberg [1979: 59] uses the term *self-concept* as synonymous with identity: the individual's fundamental frame of reference, the foundation on which almost all his or her actions are predicated. Rosenberg advances the understanding of self-concept by treating it as three-dimensional: development of an autonomous identity, maintenance of a stable identity, and establishment of levels of self-esteem.

In the following discussion, the terms *identity* and *self-concept* are used interchangeably.

Development of Autonomous Identity: Necessary Conditions

As mentioned above, the growing child must establish a self that is separate from the family. In adolescence, this becomes especially important as it is a major step toward attaining maturity. Certain conditions are essential for the development of an autonomous identity.

Basic Attachment. The achievement of an autonomous identity in adolescence is a continuation of a process that begins in infancy. It cannot take place without the separation-individuation process, as described by Mahler: "The child achieves separate functioning in the presence of, and with the emotional availability of, the mother" [1963: 3]. Developing an autonomous identity means eventually gaining autonomy from parental control and developing a personal identity that is distinct from one's family.

Continuity. Erikson emphasizes the importance of continuity in the child's experience as an important prerequisite for identity formation:

> The young person, in order to experience wholeness, must feel a progressive continuity between that which he has come to be during the long years of childhood and that which he promises to become in the anticipated future; between that which he perceives himself to be and that which he perceives others to see in him and to expect of him. [1964: 91]

Ideally, children move gradually toward independence from a base of secure attachment to their parents, and continuity is sustained by their experience as part of a developing family.

Adequate Environment. Young people require certain basic conditions to negotiate the task of forming a secure identity separate from their families: a stable family base, a supportive external structure, and the opportunity to regress when they feel overwhelmed.

In terms of stability, young people need their parents as role models: the parent-child relationship is the "genetic link that reaches back into the past and ahead into the future" [Laird 1979: 177]. If one parent is absent, the youth needs a positive representation of that parent with which to identify. Ideally, families also provide stability by tolerating and containing the young person's struggle for independence. In seeking an identity, many adolescents continually test their parents' limits and question their values. If a new partner has joined a single-parent family, clashes may develop when the adolescent rejects this new source of authority, and the parent may be forced to mediate between the partner and the adolescent. Parents who are insecure or over-stressed may react to these pressures by "extruding"* the adolescent. Families with sufficient income can seek temporary relief through socially acceptable means, such as camp, holidays, or boarding school. Low-income families do not have these supports and are more likely to turn to a placement agency for a solution.

Adolescents require family structures that are flexible enough to allow them increasing independence, while providing some external limits to help them develop internal controls. In effect,

---

* *Extruding* is a neutral term, to denote that parents may initiate placement of adolescents without emotionally rejecting them. They view placement as a solution to a family crisis and may have strong positive feelings for their child despite their evident frustration or anger.

the home provides a secure base from which adolescents can gradually test their own readiness for independence, and a source of comfort and support for them when the outside world becomes too stressful. Adolescents must also be allowed regressive, narcissistic periods to mobilize their mental and emotional resources [Solnit 1982]. Ideally, they will have a home environment that makes minimal psychological demands, leaving them to expend their energy on the challenges of peers and school.

Complications for Adolescents Who Require Child Welfare Services

Adolescents whose families seek placement for them often have difficulty achieving an autonomous identity because they have not had the necessary stability and structure for their psychological development. They may be members of a disadvantaged minority, they may prematurely assume adult roles, or they may identify with an adolescent subculture. More damaging still, they may not have completed basic separation/individuation (unintegrated children). All these complications can give rise to special needs.

Membership in a Disadvantaged Minority. Youths from disadvantaged racial or ethnic groups may incorporate negative views from the larger society into their self-concepts. They may adopt behaviors connected with the dominant culture's negative stereotypes of their group. Alternatively, they may choose to ignore or reject the racial aspect of their identity, denying that they are different from peers who do not share their minority status. This is particularly likely if the youths are in care and have little contact with their own racial or ethnic group. Assuming that racial or ethnic origins are an important part of identity, youths must gain understanding and acceptance of the group in which they have primary membership.

Premature Assumption of Adult Roles. Children may take on adult responsibilities because of family conditions such as poverty, parental addiction, or parental absence. They may become caregivers for younger children or for a parent; or they may become emotionally enmeshed across generational boundaries, that is, there is insufficient autonomy of each family member and the adolescent experiences the parent's feelings as his own [Hartman & Laird 1983]. A typical example is that of a sole-support mother who turns to her oldest child for help with her work and her concerns. The family may function fairly well in the short-term: over time, however, the youth is likely to want additional freedom and may join an adolescent subculture; or the mother may bring in an adult partner and displace the youth. The resulting conflicts may lead to extrusion of the youth from the family, but the emotional enmeshment remains, and the youth's development of an autonomous identity is hampered.

Adolescents who are enmeshed in their families principally need their level of responsibility to be reduced gradually. Commonly, expectations change too suddenly, either because the parent finds a new partner or the adolescent rebels. This throws the family into disequilibrium. Both parents and youths need encouragement to change their roles gradually: the parent who has needed the youth's support will be ambivalent about giving it up; and the youth may resist giving up a large part of his identity. Adequate supports for the family must be found from other sources to fill the gap left behind as the enmeshed adolescent becomes independent.

Identification with an Adolescent Subculture. Most adolescents seek to join their peers in group activity that expresses their common needs and interests, and asserts their freedom from adult authority. For youths who have limited access to socially approved activities or who feel excluded from mainstream society, peer group activity may be explicitly antisocial, characterized by such activities as serious substance abuse or criminal offenses. These activities are attractive to youths who feel undervalued by teachers and socially accepted peers. A subculture of other alienated youths offers them acceptance and identity. In their desire to belong, adolescents tend to merge with the peer group and to accept its frame of reference. Because such adolescents are not ready to evaluate and accept responsibility for their own actions, they are not able to develop an autonomous identity.

Adolescents who join an antisocial subculture usually create conflict in their homes because their behavior offends parental values; this may cause their parents to extrude them. These adolescents have to be reassured that they have not been completely rejected by their families. It is important that the family be helped to identify and reinforce the mutual love and respect that tends to become buried in the turmoil of adolescent rebellion.

Incomplete Separation/Individuation. As described earlier, children who lack an adequate primary care experience cannot move ahead with normal developmental tasks. Unless they have a long-term compensatory experience, they become unintegrated adolescents, unable to trust or relate to others as individuals with needs of their own. As adolescents, they are expected to begin developing an independent identity, yet they lack a secure family relationship from which to begin seeking independence.

The best chance for these adolescents would seem to be a compensatory experience in which they can regress to an earlier stage and learn basic trust with a dependable parenting figure. Unfortunately, the regular foster care system is unlikely to offer an environment in which regression is acceptable. Thus, unintegrated adolescents in care tend to create chaos in their efforts to seek independence without the necessary foundations for this big step.

Self-Esteem

Identity and self-esteem are inextricably related: adolescents must know who they are before they can evaluate themselves. Yet it is important to consider the two concepts separately: placement may have a crucial effect on self-esteem, but the person's identity may remain unchanged in most respects. The adolescent's level of self-esteem is dependent upon—and varies with—reflected appraisals, social comparisons, her sense of competence, and feelings of belonging [Rosenberg 1979].

Reflected Appraisals. Developing children base their self-esteem on the judgments of significant others. There are several sources for these "reflected appraisals": how significant others view the child, how the child believes the others view her, and the attitude of the community as a whole [Rosenberg 1979]. Significant others are likely to be parents; research shows that about 50% of children expect their parents' judgments of their personal characteristics to be more valid than their own [Rosenberg 1979]. As for the attitude of the wider community, judgments about young people tend to be partly based on the reputation of their parents. Research indicates, moreover, that most children feel personally attacked by any criticism of their families [Rosenberg 1979].

Social Comparisons and Competence. Social comparisons—in which people compare themselves with referent individuals and groups—are another aspect of self-esteem [Rosenberg 1979]. Adolescents tend to make these comparisons with others in their immediate home and school environment.

A sense of competence is necessary to a positive self-evaluation. For developing children, this comes mainly from their successes in negotiating the world around them. In the early years, the security of children's attachment to their main caregiver is an important factor: infants who can rely on their caregivers will use them as a base for exploration, will develop their motor skills, and will sense themselves to be effective [Sroufe 1983].

For adolescents, the basis for a positive experience is more complex. Those from homes that are disadvantaged by poverty or minority status are likely to fall behind in school and to encounter social discrimination. These experiences will undermine their self-esteem, even though the adolescents may be accepted within their own families. Some adolescents try to compensate for failure and social rejection by joining a peer group in which success is based on antisocial behavior. Standards for behavior within the group may be the reverse of those in mainstream society: that is, the more antisocial the group members' behavior, the more status they achieve.

Feeling of Belonging. Finally, self-esteem depends on feeling that one has a place in the world. For children and youths, the main source of this feeling is being part of a family. David, a teenager in foster care, expressed his feelings in a letter to his social worker after a reunion with "long-lost" relatives [Laird 1979: 186]. He had come into care at 13 when his grandparents died, and wrote about that experience, "I never felt that I belonged anywhere." After meeting his other grandparents and relatives, he wrote, "I feel as though I belong now, and that I am somebody and that is the best feeling anyone could have in this situation" [Laird 1979: 186].

Effect of Placement in Foster Care on Identity and Self-Esteem

Placement in foster care may be expected to have a powerful impact on identity formation, self-esteem, and stability of self-concept.

Interruption of Identity Development

Loss of Basic Framework. Placement interrupts the task of achieving autonomy from the family by abruptly moving the young person away from his basic source of identification. The placed adolescent no longer has a secure home base from which he can gradually test his ability to cope independently in society. Furthermore, the move breaks the continuity between the youth's past and future: there is no longer one person who shares important memories and can help him to develop a continuous personal history. As Laird so poignantly expresses it, the young person in care has been "torn from the biological and symbolic context of his identity," in a way that creates a "jagged tear in (its) fabric" [1979: 175–176].

The interruption of identity formation is likely to undermine the success of placement. As pointed out by Erikson [1963: 263–264], the ability to form intimate relationships depends on a secure identity. Adolescents who have been moved away from the main source of their identity may be expected to have great difficulty forming a meaningful relationship with another family. Charles, 15, expressed this feeling as he was being moved from a placement after three months at the request of the foster carers [Children's Aid Society of Metropolitan Toronto 1984]. He said, "We didn't really dislike each other or like each other." In other words, little feeling was expressed between Charles and his foster carers. His strong feelings were reserved for his mother: he felt guilty when he remembered their arguments, which had sometimes reached the point of physical conflict.

Reaction to Loss. Youths in care lose the opportunity for a continuing experience through which they can evaluate their parents' life-style and values. To fill this void, they may try to recreate their parents' lives: "in prolonged placements, the child may be even more prone to duplicate destructive family patterns in his or her own adult interpersonal and family relationships" [Laird 1979: 191]. This reaction occurs even when children seem to have adequate placements and good supports. The less information an adolescent has about his family members, the more likely he is to try to recreate them: a youth will often "act out destructively in a way which reflects the few facts he may have about his hidden or lost parents, or even worse, on the basis of his fantasies about the lost object" [Laird 1979: 185]. Youths who have been part of an alienated subculture generally lose this support when they enter care; in fact, it may be a goal of placement to separate them from "bad companions." If the group has been an important part of their identity, they may go to great lengths to be with their friends. Alternatively, they may try to join a new peer group. More proactive youths may create their own antisocial subculture in the new home, especially in a group environment.

Risk to Unintegrated Adolescents. Adolescents who are unintegrated are at greatest risk of discontinuity, because they have little sense of identity as a base for adapting to change. They often have a history of agency care from an early age, with repeated failed foster placements [Barker 1978: 3]. The eventual placement of last resort tends to be residential care, either an institution or a group home. This is unlikely to meet the adolescent's need for a compensatory experience with a caregiver she may begin to trust. Considering the likelihood that unintegrated adolescents will have a series of homes, it seems particularly important that they maintain ties with their families to provide a basis for identity.

Role Loss for Enmeshed Adolescents. Adolescents who have been assuming adult responsibility in their families lose this role when they are moved. To the degree that this responsibility is an important part of their identity, they may resist giving it up. In a group treatment program with youths in care, children as young as age six had been "parenting" their parents, and expressed a sense of continuing responsibility [Palmer 1990].

Isolation from Minority Group. Minority youths entering care may lose touch with the cultural, racial, or ethnic group that provided them with an identity, as foster homes are usually located within the dominant culture. Although legislation and policy have recognized the value of cultural continuity, and adoptive homes are usually sought within the child's own culture, little attention is given to cultural continuity in foster care. For example, an agency located in a community with many Portuguese immigrant families continued to place children in traditional Canadian families, where no attention was given to the food or other customs of Portuguese families. Anna, age 12, expressed her longing for familiar food, but her worker and foster mother expected her to adapt to the foster family [Palmer 1990].

Native Indians in care may feel a particular void in their lives from their loss of cultural identity because they often have little opportunity for contact with their own people. John, 18, could not recall his family and had always lived among Caucasians, yet he showed a wish to identify with his origins. When discussing political resistance by Mohawk Indians in Quebec, he said with enthusiasm: "It gave us back our pride!"

Lowered Self-Esteem

Placement in foster care may be expected to depress a youth's self-esteem, in terms of reflected appraisals, social comparisons, sense of competence, and need to belong.

Reflected Appraisals. Youths living apart from their families are likely to feel they have been rejected by the very persons whose opinions they most value. Feelings of rejection and confusion may be counteracted by ongoing family contact, and by family interviews to deal with conflicts that may have caused the move.

Another issue is the reflection on children in care of others' views about their families. Many foster carers find it difficult to accept the child's biological parents, and the wider community tends to avoid acknowledging the existence of another family while a youth is in foster care. As noted earlier, children in care are likely to construe negative appraisals of their family as including themselves. Given the lack of acceptance of their parents, it will be difficult for these children to feel accepted by foster carers or the wider society.

Social Comparisons. To the extent that self-esteem depends on social comparisons, children in care are likely to feel inferior to their new reference group. In comparison to other children in the foster family, neighborhood, and school, children in care are usually from lower socioeconomic circumstances.

They are the newcomers trying to fit in, and are likely to be marginalized because they are different. If they are from a disadvantaged minority, the comparisons may be even more discrepant. Pat, 20, a West Indian formerly in care, recalled being taunted by students at her high school, who called her a "foster home hippie." In her group home, she was the only Black, and was the target of racist slurs [Malcolm 1990].

Sense of Competence. Adolescence is a time of change, requiring energy if the youth is to succeed at school or work, and to be accepted by his peers. A move to a totally new environment places immense pressure on adolescents to adapt. They have to relate to significant others—and to a larger community—whose norms and values are new to them. This diverts their energy from normal developmental tasks, and their achievements are likely to suffer. At the very least, they need the people around them to acknowledge these pressures.

Adolescents entering care may feel they have failed in their own families. Admission to care is often precipitated, at least in part, by behavior that the youth's family cannot tolerate. Thus the youth is at risk of feeling guilty about the past, which will tend to lower her self-esteem. Again, family discussions can be helpful; an understanding of the past should help to minimize guilt.

Need to Belong. Youths in care do not belong to the foster carers in the same way the carers' own children do. Vivian lived in the same foster family from infancy, and her foster carers adopted her when she reached majority and foster payments ended. Despite this evidence of acceptance, she continued to feel insecure and often told the foster carers of her longing to be like their own daughter.

The youth's status within his own family is threatened by his absence, especially if the family remains intact after he leaves.

> [When] the child is emotionally and physically distanced, the family system forms a new homeostatic balance without his presence...when the child returns, he may find the

family has adapted to his absence in a variety of ways which may be experienced as further rejection and isolation. [Laird 1979: 199]

Youths in care can probably never completely belong to a new family, so it is important for them to have contact with people to whom they are tied through blood.

Instability of Self-Concept

A change in people's environment changes their self-concept [Rosenberg 1979]. Youths in care may be expected to have unstable self-concepts because they experience changes—sometimes a great many—in significant others and comparison groups.

Uncertainty. Many youths in care have little or no contact with their families. This leaves them feeling uncertain about how their families view them. Uncertainty about foster status has been found to be associated with poor adjustment in foster homes [Weinstein 1960; Holman 1965]. Uncertainty about their acceptability in a new environment is magnified when customs and values are different from those in the youths' own cultures; they may not be able to interpret signs of acceptance or rejection.

Dissonance. Differences in social class between biological families and foster carers may be expected to contribute to identity confusion, as dissonant socioeconomic environments are associated with instability of self-concept [Rosenberg 1979]. Marked differences in cultural values will add to the confusion: if a child belongs to two subgroups with different values, such as the foster family and her own family, the likelihood of confusion, tension, and discord increases [Santa-Barbara et al. 1981: 55]. Jennifer, 13, entered care following a revelation of earlier sexual abuse; her mother, who had regular contact with her, gave her a book about personal safety that made reference to "safe sex." Jennifer's foster carers were strongly religious and had fairly narrow views on appropriate behavior for adolescent girls. They objected strenuously to the book, telling Jennifer never to bring it into their house again [Legere 1990]. Their reaction was damaging to the self-esteem of both Jennifer and her mother.

Dissociation. Youths who perceive that their parents are not respected by their foster carers may try to dissociate themselves from their families, to avoid being similarly classified. Research indicates that when children belong to reference groups of which they are not proud, they tend to exclude these from their self-concepts [Rosenberg 1979: 188]. Youths who cope in this way may be left without a sense of membership in any family, and the instability of their identity is likely to increase.

Adolescents in care are therefore vulnerable to several influences that may cause instability in their self-concept: a completely new set of relationships, dissonance between two groups in which they are members, and possible temptation to dissociate themselves from their biological families.

Implications of Attachment and Separation Theory for Foster Care

Attachment and separation theory can help us to understand what happens to a child in foster placement, while acknowledging the differences between foster placement and other common forms of separation. First, the theory helps us to anticipate and interpret children's responses and needs, and the effect that placement will have on their development. Second, it yields indicators for parents, foster carers, and social workers seeking to lessen the trauma of placement.

Children's Reactions to Placement

Do children placed in foster care show the same reactions as children in other common separation experiences? The children in the Robertsons' study [1971] went through the expected phases of response when they were placed in care while their mothers were confined for childbirth, but these children were very young (under two years of age) and the separations occurred because of a normal life event. When foster care takes place because of family breakdown, there is little published evidence to indicate that children show depression or despair; instead, their emotional responses seem to be blunted.

From theory, we know that young children experiencing common separation experiences progress through recognized stages of protest, despair, and depression; they do not generally become detached. Even those placed in minimal disruption foster care during their mother's confinement did not move into premature detachment, and were able to adapt easily to reunion on her return [Robertson & Robertson 1971]. Can we expect similar responses in children being moved into foster placement?

The difference between foster placement and the separations in most of the above studies is significant—the latter involved children from homes that were assumed to be adequate, while foster placement generally results from family breakdown in homes that are considered inadequate by community standards. Nevertheless, children who have lived with their families since birth will usually accept their home conditions–whatever they may be—as normal. Accordingly, we should expect them to react to separation by moving through the stages of protest, despair, and depression.* How can we explain, then, the apparent absence of these reactions in children being moved into foster care?

We do have some indication that children in typical placement situations make an initial protest as they are removed from their parents.

> All [child protection workers] who have been involved when children are removed from a home have witnessed how youngsters cling even to abusing parents...[and have]

---

* An exception to this would be adolescents who have requested placement; they would probably not protest although they might show despair and depression about the separation.

seen children run away from adequate foster homes to inadequate parental homes. [Cole 1984]

Beyond the initial protest at leaving home, however, no empirical studies have shown that regular foster placement elicits clear responses of despair and depression in children. Nor have despair and depression been explicitly seen or reported in the author's experience in several placement agencies as a worker, supervisor, and staff trainer. The protest described by Cole tended to take place only in the parents' presence. As the farewell usually occurred in the child's home, the parents were soon left behind, and the child tended to lapse into a "frozen" silence. Foster carers would usually report, over the next few days, that the child was "settling in well," with no apparent signs of upset.

The lack of emotional response by children in regular foster care could be viewed as premature detachment. It did not persist when contact with parents was resumed. With regular parental contact, the freezing would thaw and the children's underlying feelings would emerge: they would resist separating from their parents at the end of a visit or would show disturbed behavior around the time of contact. Experience with these children, therefore, suggests that a child's apparent lack of concern about separation is likely to be a defensive reaction.

When children had no parental contact, their detachment seemed to persist. They would often have a honeymoon period in the new home, lasting four to six weeks; when this ended, some children changed their behavior quite abruptly, acting out rebelliously or withdrawing from the family. Rebellious behavior could be a belated form of protest, and withdrawal could be a sign of depression. This behavior may reflect children's detachment from their separation reactions, as they were not giving any direct expression to the sadness or anger they might be expected to feel at the loss of their families. In the author's experience, however, neither foster carers nor workers made any interpretation that connected the children's emerging behavior with their separation experiences.

From the foregoing discussion, it seems that children who have no family contact are at greatest risk of becoming prematurely detached from others as their way of handling the pain of separation. A young woman, looking back on her experience of moving from one foster home to another at age five, recalled hiding her feelings: "Tears may be denied, so that the child hides the torment" [Hinton 1978: 10]. She wrote that her caregivers did not recognize her feelings, and that foster carers should look for the child's "despondency" and for the "fabrication."

Why do children being moved into foster placements move so quickly to detachment, without demonstrating the stages of protest, despair, and depression found in other common separation experiences? A basic condition for the free expression of feelings is the child's ability to admit them to consciousness. Losing her parents and being moved to a strange place by strange people may be so overwhelming to a child that she has to deny her feelings. Five-year-old Charlene was placed in foster care after the death of her parents in a car accident while she was in the car. It was only during the last of five play therapy sessions, that is, when she knew this was her last opportunity, that she was able to express anger and sadness about this traumatic experience [Steinhauer 1991]. The therapist noted that Charlene never cried, even though he and her worker had both cried in her presence, reacting to the tragedy of her loss. He encouraged her to cry, and concluded that she was held back by "the enormity of her grief" [Steinhauer 1991].

Most children entering care do not lose their parents to death, but their sense of being abandoned may be just as traumatic as Charlene's. Thus, we can hypothesize that children may be too overwhelmed by placement and its implications to admit their feelings to consciousness. Let us consider the differences between foster placement and other common separations.

First, foster placement is likely to be more traumatic than

other forms of separation, particularly as it involves people and places that are unfamiliar. Second, children admitted to care have usually experienced stressful situations in their homes leading up to the separation. When a family is breaking up, the environment is likely to be one of crisis, loss of control, and uncertainty about the future.

Third, children entering agency care may already be insecure in their attachments to their parents. Often this comes about because the family lives in an unsupportive environment. If the family has inadequate income and/or has a marginalized status in society, the parents may be overwhelmed, disorganized, and inconsistent in meeting their children's needs for physical and emotional nurturance. As noted earlier, children whose family attachments are insecure may be expected to have more difficulty in tolerating separation.

Fourth, related to the third, children who are being placed usually have low self-esteem, arising from unreliable or abusive parenting and the low status of their families in the larger community. Low self-esteem will cause these children to doubt the validity of their feelings. Furthermore, past experiences will have taught them that they have little power to influence their environment. They will see no point in expressing their feelings directly; this will accomplish nothing and only make them increasingly aware of their own pain.

Finally, a number of children entering care have been abused (physically, sexually, and/or emotionally) in their families and are suffering from posttraumatic stress disorder. Their reactions to the environment, even before separation, will be characterized by anxiety, hyperarousal to perceived threats, and affective numbing [Fine 1989].

All these influences tend to push children into premature detachment from their feelings about separation, and they bury their ambivalent reactions of yearning for and anger toward their parents. One consequence is that these unresolved feelings prevent them from placing trust in new caregivers.

Implications of Theory for the Development
of Children in Placement

Loss of parents through a move into foster care may be expected to interfere with a number of basic developmental processes. These can be examined in terms of progress through Erikson's developmental tasks: the capacity to trust, to undertake independent learning, to focus on school and peer relationships, and to seek an independent identity. As these tasks are based on the evolution of parent-child relationships, children living apart from their parents will have difficulty in completing them.

The profound importance to an infant of developing a trusting relationship with a particular caregiver is shown by the institutionalized infants studied by Spitz and Wolfe [1946]. When they were deprived of their mothers, many of these infants died or showed drastic retardation in their development. These observations were supported by the marked improvement in children when their mothers returned. Children placed in foster care may not have a relationship of trust with their biological parents, or their trust may have been deeply shaken by an abrupt separation. Thus, the basic ingredients for developing or regaining a capacity to trust are missing.

In terms of independent learning, Mahler's theory of separation-individuation and Bowlby's observations assume conditions under which young children are left to make the first move toward independence. When separation is forced on children, however, their natural initiative toward independent learning is likely to be blocked by separation anxiety. These effects were shown by the behavior of young children in the research of Marvin [1977] and Ainsworth et al. [1978]: when children were deprived of their mothers' presence, they stopped exploring their environment until their mothers returned.

Very young children, who are often assumed to be the easiest to "transplant," are actually the most vulnerable to damage when separated from their parents. Separation is likely to interrupt their progress through developmental stages in terms of psychological individuation and exploration of the environment. School-aged children have the tasks of achieving at school and learning how to relate to their peers, challenges that require a great deal of psychic energy. If we place children at this age in a totally strange environment, we require them to focus their energy on reorienting themselves to a new world. We may also be increasing their emotional dependence on their families, as "physical and emotional distancing promotes rather than weakens psychological dependency" [Laird 1979: 191].

Who Are the Most Vulnerable Children?

Theory and research offer some knowledge that contradicts traditional agency beliefs about which children are most vulnerable to damage from separation. This knowledge relates to age, relationships with parents, and placement history. Agencies and foster carers, in the author's experience, favor moving children earlier rather than later. They believe that infants and toddlers are more adaptable than older children to a change in caregiver. Yet theory indicates that children age seven months to three years are at greatest risk of being damaged by separation. Children over three years of age have a better developed internalization of their mother's image, so separation is less threatening to them, especially if the internalized image is reinforced by regular contact during placement.

In terms of parent-child relationships, the author has often encountered an expectation in workers that children with poor or ambivalent relationships will be grateful for "replacement" parents, and free to engage with them. This expectation is contradicted by the theory that these children will be unable to trust. Children who have had good relationships with their parents, however, are somewhat able to maintain a positive, integrated image of them during separation, decreasing their vulnerability. Furthermore, the quality of the child's early relationship with the primary caregiver influences the quality of the relationships she develops with her secondary caregivers [Bloom-Feshbach et al. 1987].

The child who is being placed for the first time tends to elicit the greatest concern from agencies and workers, who are aware of his vulnerability. Yet research indicates that the damage from changes in placement is cumulative; thus, the child most at risk is the one who has been moved before. Each successive change probably causes children to bury their feelings more deeply from view.

The Roles of Parents, Foster Carers, and Workers in Modifying the Deleterious Effects of Placement

From the above discussion, the salient considerations are that children tend to repress their feelings about separation and become prematurely detached; that those children assumed to be least vulnerable are actually likely to be most damaged by separation; and that unresolved issues will hinder the children's future development. What can we distill from these considerations to guide the adults most involved with the children—their parents, foster carers, and workers?

All adults involved in the child's placement must collaborate to provide conditions that will allow the child to experience and express his underlying feelings. These feelings are most likely to be accessible if the child's fear is manageable, if the child can trust the person with him, and if the child can feel that he has some power in the situation, that is, that his feelings are valid and that expressing them may have some impact on others.

Parents. From Bowlby's observations of separation anxiety, we know that young children are frightened by unknown people and strange surroundings, especially when both conditions exist together [1973]. These are the conditions encountered by most children being placed in foster care, as only a minority are accompanied by their parents [Kufeldt et al. 1989]. We also know that a supportive environment can reduce children's fear. Parental accompaniment to a new home can remove the frightening condition of unknown people. Laboratory studies have confirmed that the presence of the child's mother is tremendously reassuring to the child in a strange situation [Ainsworth et al. 1978].

Parents can also reduce their children's fear by preparing them for the separation. This tends to be done routinely when the reason for separation is socially acceptable, such as the parents' work, holidays, or illness. When a child requires placement for her own protection, however, it is usually a reflection on her parents, and it is more difficult for them to prepare her for placement. To give children some sense of control over their lives, parents should tell them the truth about why they are being moved, and share everything they know about future plans.

The foregoing discussion concerns mainly younger children, but older children have even more potential to benefit from verbal preparation for placement. As discussed earlier, children older than age three have a lessened need for the actual presence of a parent, especially if they are secure about parental love and approval [Provence 1987]. Parents should reassure older children that they are neither rejected nor is the placement their fault; the best way to do this is to explain fully why they are being placed.

Finally, the prerequisite of trust in an adult that enables children to share their feelings can best be met by parents. The very young child, as we know, has a small circle of trust that does not extend to strangers. This is well illustrated in the case of Bill, age three, who was being placed for adoption [Kirk 1981]. Bill did not express his real feelings until many months after placement, when he was sharing a particularly close moment with his adoptive father. Then he suddenly said he wanted to "go home" (back to the previous foster home). Bill's placement with the adoptive family had been abrupt: when his worker brought him for a second preplacement visit, she announced that this would be the placement, and that Bill would not be returning to the foster home. This sudden change in plans was the worker's reaction to remarks made to Bill by the father in the foster family, who was resisting the separation. The worker was upset and decided not to take Bill back to the foster home. She appeared to be trying to protect Bill, but he cried the next day when told by his adoptive family that he would not be going back to the foster home as planned. Then he apparently buried his feelings until he had enough trust in his adoptive family to reveal them. Accordingly, he was given a good-bye visit with his former foster carers and appeared to benefit from it.

Children are always in a relatively weak power position vis-à-vis adults; they will feel powerless in the placement process unless they feel they can influence the adults who do have the power. For this, they must have some trust in the adult; if their parents remove themselves from the placement process at an early point, it reduces the child's sense of power to influence what occurs.

Foster Carers. It is difficult for adults working with child placement to interpret the child's reactions. The most vulnerable children are the least likely to express their feelings directly. As foster carers naturally make judgments about children from their behavior, it is important for them to recognize that the appearance of emotional detachment in a child is probably a natural reaction to separation, not a personality trait. Foster carers tend to underestimate the degree of children's pain at separation, because they want to believe the child is happy in their home. For example, the foster carers for Charlene, age five, whose parents had just died, reported that she was doing well in their home, attributing this to the warm environment they provided [Steinhauer 1991]. In fact, play therapy revealed that Charlene was hiding her underlying pain; when Steinhauer helped her to express and play out some of her pain, she was able to begin facing her loss.

Foster carers have to recognize that they cannot replace the child's parents. Otherwise, they may try to have parental contact reduced on the basis that it upsets the child. They must also be careful not to abuse the great power they have over the agency; workers are likely to accept the foster carers' request for reduced family contact, even against their own judgment, because they are so afraid of losing a foster home and having to re-place the child.

Workers. The worker is responsible for managing parent-child separation in a manner that is sensitive to the child's psychological readiness and that builds in as much environmental support as possible. In view of the crisis-oriented nature of child protection work, workers may think they lack the time and skill needed to deal with children's feelings; yet they may create more work for themselves by ignoring children's needs and risking subsequent placement breakdown.

Attention to the child's psychological readiness involves ensuring that the parents have verbally prepared the child for separation, in the ways described above; if this is impossible, then the worker must do some compensatory work. It is never too late for children to hear a full and truthful explanation of the reason for their separation from their parents, as we have learned from adult adoptees. The worker should also arrange to include foster carers in such discussions, thereby opening the way for the child to talk further about the separation in the new home.

The findings from the minimal disruption foster care experiment provide indicators for building a supportive environment—reducing strangeness by making sure that children have familiar transitional objects, and arranging preplacement visits, parental accompaniment, and regular contact. It is also the worker's task to help parents deal with their own feelings about placement, so that they can then help their children. Otherwise, parents who feel discouraged or guilty about placing their children may behave in ways that undermine the placement.

A move away from his own family threatens a child's identity.

After such a break, the child's "ongoing task will always be to reweave the jagged tear in the fabric of his identity, to make himself whole again" [Germain 1979: 176].

As for self-esteem, children in care require access to their biological roots to sustain a sense of their personal significance [Colon 1978]. Ideally, this access will come from continuing family contact. If this is not possible, it is the worker's responsibility to help children to fill the gaps in their personal history.

In summary, children entering foster care do not usually go through the expected stages of separation, because the trauma of placement is so overwhelming. More often, they move into premature detachment from their feelings, expressing their feelings indirectly through disturbed behavior. In good placement practice, adults will collaborate to provide an environment that keeps children's anxieties to a manageable level. It is vital to facilitate children's expression of their underlying feelings, preferably to their parents. If children feel free to ask questions, and if they receive honest answers, there will be fewer unknowns to make them anxious. If children have continuing family contact, they will have a chance to complete the developmental tasks that revolve around their parents. Without contact and sharing of information, we can expect from theory, research, and experience that children will bury their feelings and move prematurely to detachment, thereby damaging their capacity for future relationships.

Identity and self-esteem are intimately linked with family connections. Children who have been uprooted need help in maintaining links with their families, either in person or through the sharing of information to help them understand their own origins and history.

References

Ainsworth, M.D.S., Blehar, M.C., Waters, E., and Wall, S. (1978). *Patterns of attachment: A psychological study of the strange situation*. Hillsdale, NJ: Erlbaum.

Balbernie, R. (1974.) Unintegration, integration and level of ego functioning as the determinants of planned "cover therapy" of unit task
and of placement. *Journal of the Association of Workers for Maladjusted Children, 2*, 6–46.

Barker, P. (1978). The impossible child: Some approaches to treatment.
In P.D. Steinhauer (Ed.), The Laidlaw Foundation workshop on the
"impossible" child: An overview. *Canadian Psychiatric Journal, 23*, 1–21.

Bloom-Feshbach, J., & Bloom-Feshbach, S. (1987). *The psychology of
separation and loss.* San Francisco: Jossey-Bass.

Bowlby, J. (1961). Processes of mourning. *International Journal of Psychoanalysis, 42*, 317–340.

Bowlby, J. (1969). *Attachment and loss: Vol. I. Attachment.* New York: Basic
Books.

Bowlby, J. (1973). *Attachment and loss: Vol. II. Separation.* New York: Basic
Books.

Bowlby, J. (1980). *Attachment and loss: Vol. III. Loss: Sadness and depression.* New York: Basic Books.

Bowlby, J. (1982). Attachment and loss: Retrospect and prospect.
American Journal of Orthopsychiatry, 52, 664–678.

Children's Aid Society of Metropolitan Toronto. (1984). *Tear on the
dotted line.* Toronto, ON: TV Ontario (videotape).

Cole, E. (1984). Foreword. In K. Blumenthal & A. Weinberg (Eds.),
Establishing parent involvement in foster care agencies (pp. xi–xii).
New York: Child Welfare League of America.

Colon, F. (1978). Family ties and child placement. *Family Process, 17*,
289–312.

Egeland, B., & Sroufe, L. A. (1981). Attachment and early maltreatment.
Child Development, 52, 44–52.

Erikson, E.H. (1963). *Childhood and society.* New York: W.W. Norton.

Erikson, E.H. (1964). *Insight and responsibility.* New York: W.W. Norton.

Farber, E. A., & Egeland, B. (1987). Abused and neglected children. In E.
J. Anthony and B. J. Cohler (Eds.), *The invulnerable child* (pp. 253–
289). New York: Guilford Press.

Festinger, T. (1983). *No one ever asked us...A postscript to foster care.* New
York: Columbia University Press.

Fine, P. (1989). *The emotional functioning of children in the foster care system* (unpublished paper, Creighton-Nebraska Department of Psychiatry).

Fraiberg, S. (1969). Libidinal object constancy and mental representation. *Psychoanalytic Study of the Child, 24*, 9–47.

Germain, C. (1979). Editor's introduction to J. Laird, An ecological approach to child welfare: Issues of family identity and continuity. In C. Germain (Ed.), *People and environments* (pp. 174–209). New York: Columbia University Press.

Goldfarb, W. (1945). Psychological privation in infancy and subsequent adjustment. *American Journal of Orthopsychiatry, 15*, 247–255.

Goldfarb, W. (1955). Emotional and intellectual consequences of psychologic deprivation in infancy: A reevaluation. In P. Hoch & J. Zubin (Eds.), *Psychopathology of childhood* (pp. 105–119). Orlando, FL: Grune & Stratton.

Hartman, A., & Laird, J. (1983). *Family-centered practice*. New York: Free Press.

Hinton, S. (1978, March). On being a foster child. *Journal of the Ontario Association of Children's Aid Societies, 21*, 9–10.

Holman, R. (1965). The foster child and self knowledge. *Case Conference 12*, 295–298.

Kirk, D. (1981). *Adoptive kinship: A modern institution in need of reform*. Toronto, ON: Butterworth.

Kufeldt, K., Armstrong, J., & Dorosh, M. (1989). In care, in contact? In J. Hudson & Burt Galaway (Eds.), *The state as parent* (pp. 355–368). Dordrecht, Netherlands: Kluwer Academic Publishers.

Legere, S. (1990). *Interview between a birth mother and the author*. Hamilton, ON: McMaster University (videotape).

Lieberman, A.F. (1987). Separation in infancy and early childhood: Contributions of attachment theory and psychoanalysis. In J. Bloom-Feshbach, S. Bloom-Feshbach, & Associates (Eds.), *The psychology of separation and loss* (pp. 109–135). San Francisco: Jossey-Bass.

Mahler, M.S. (1963). Certain aspects of the separation-individuation phase. *Psychoanalytic Quarterly, 32*, 1–14.

Mahler, M.S., Pine, F., & Bergman, A. (1975). *The psychological birth of the human infant: Symbiosis and individuation*. New York: Basic Books.

Malcolm, P. (1990). *A former foster child speaks of her experiences*. Videotape by author at Children's Aid Society of Metropolitan Toronto.

Marvin, R.S. (1977). An ethological-cognitive model for the attenuation of mother-child attachment behavior. In T.M. Alloway, L. Krames, & P. Pliner (Eds.), *Advances in the study of communications and affect: Vol. 3. Attachment behavior* (pp. 25–60). New York: Plenum.

Palmer, S. (1990). Group treatment of children to reduce separation conflicts associated with placement breakdown. *Child Welfare, 69*, 227–233.

Provence, S. (1987). "Psychoanalytic Views of Separation in Infancy and Early Childhood." In J. Bloom-Feshbach, S. Bloom-Feshbach, & Associates (Eds.), *The psychology of separation and loss* (pp. 87–108). San Francisco: Jossey-Bass.

Robertson, J., & Bowlby, J. (1952). Responses of young children to separation from their mothers. *Courrier du Centre International de L'Enfance, 2*, 131–142.

Robertson, J., & Robertson, J. (1971). Young children in brief separation: A fresh look. *Psychoanalytic Study of the Child, 26*, 264–315.

Rosenberg, M. (1979). *Conceiving the self*. New York: Basic Books.

Rutter, M. (1972). *Maternal deprivation reassessed*. Harmondsworth, London: Penguin Books.

Rutter, M. (1979). Maternal deprivation, 1972–1978: New findings, new concepts, new approaches. *Child Development, 50*, 283–305.

Santa-Barbara, J., Steinhauer, P., & Skinner, H. (1981). *The process model of family functioning*. Unpublished report, Toronto, ON.

Solnit, A.J. (1982). Developmental perspectives on self and object constancy. *Psychoanalytic Study of the Child, 37*, 201–218.

Spitz, R. (1945). Hospitalism: An inquiry into the genesis of psychiatric conditions in early childhood. *Psychoanalytic Study of the Child, 1*, 53–74.

Spitz, R., & Wolf, K. (1946). Anaclitic depression: An inquiry into the genesis of psychiatric conditions in early childhood: II. *Psychoanalytic Study of the Child, 2*, 313–342.

Sroufe, L.A. (1983). Infant-caregiver attachment and patterns of adaptation in preschool: The roots of maladaptation and competence. In M. Perlmutter (Ed.), *Minnesota symposium in child psychology* (pp. 41–83). Hillsdale, NJ: Erlbaum.

Steinhauer, P. (1991). *The least detrimental alternative: A systematic guide to case planning and decision making for children in care*. Toronto, ON: University of Toronto Press.

Tizard, B., & Hodges, J. (1978). The effect of early institutional rearing on the development of eight-year-old children. *Journal of Child Psychology and Psychiatry, 19*, 99–118.

Van der Kolk, B.A. (1987). *Psychological trauma*. Washington, DC: American Psychiatric Press,

Weinstein, E.A. (1960). *The self-image of the foster child*. New York: Russell Sage Foundation.

Winnicott, D.W. (1971). *Playing and reality*. New York: Basic Books.

Yarrow, L.J. (1964). Separation from parents during early childhood. In L. Hoffman & M. Hoffman (Eds.), *Review of child development research: Vol. 1* (pp. 89–136). New York: Russell Sage Foundation.

Chapter Two
Practice and
Research Knowledge

This chapter reviews the literature on physical and psychological separation of children from their families in relation to children in care, their families, foster carers, workers, and agencies.* The main change found in the literature over time has been a reframing of child welfare problems, which were traditionally viewed as caused by the failure of individual families. Increased recognition is presently given to environmental influences, especially the context of poverty from which many children are taken into care.

The Needs of Children in Foster Care

Children in care must maintain ties with their families if they are to best counter the effects of separation from those families and maintain continuity in their lives. Children in care also need an open approach from their workers and caregivers, in terms of acknowledging their pain, providing information about their past, and encouraging them to talk about their families.

Family Ties

The theoretical importance of family connections to children's development, presented in the last chapter, is underscored by the literature on placement practice and research. Child welfare

---

* The review includes some literature as far back as the 1960s, if its contribution has not been superseded. The review covers Canadian, American, and British sources, as research findings and practice knowledge across these three countries tend to support and complement each other.

practice in North America has placed a renewed emphasis on supporting children's biological families, both to prevent unnecessary placement, and, if placement does ensue, as the preferred option in permanency planning. As the research described below will show, family relationships are basic to the ability of children to accept substitute caregivers and to the chances of the children achieving reunion with their families. Unfortunately, the literature review also indicates that accepted theory has not been well integrated with practice.

Effect of Family Ties on Children's Relationships with Foster Carers. Even children who are unlikely to be reunited with their families need workers and foster carers to help them resolve their biological family ties. Otherwise, the children's lives are likely to be complicated by feelings of loss, abandonment, rejection, and guilt.

> Placed children are...experiencing a tremendous sense of loss, which...[they] can interpret as abandonment or rejection. The children then feel devalued and guilty, internalizing the loss as their fault. It is through contact with and discussion about the family that we can in part bring the feelings to the surface, reduce the sense of guilt and abandonment, and clarify reality. [Tiddy 1986: 57]

Children are inhibited by their family ties from forming relationships with substitute caregivers because they are afraid of being disloyal [Millham et al. 1986, quoting George 1970]. In particular, children who were "parentified" in their families are likely to feel guilty about leaving their parents alone. Such worries were expressed by two (of eight) children in a group discussion of foster care: one girl explicitly did not want to leave her father "because he was on his own, and I felt responsible for him" [NFCA 1988]. Empirical support is given to this concern by the finding that alcoholism in either biological parent is associated with placement instability [Pardeck 1984].

This need to come to terms with family ties extends as well to children whose main feelings about their parents are negative:

> Children who have been abandoned or who are entangled in a mutually hostile relationship with their biological parents require help through clinical treatment to come to terms with their anger and with their fantasies about the nature of the relationship. [Fanshel et al. 1989: 476]

A child's reaction to separation is likely to be exacerbated by lack of family contact. Children who do not have ongoing contact with their families are likely to feel abandoned: "If the child is not visited, he or she might experience total abandonment and a decline in well-being" [Hess 1987: 33]. Fanshel and Shinn conclude:

> We can think of no more profound insult to a child's personality than evidence that the parent thinks so little of the relationship with him that there is no motivation to visit and see how he is faring. [1978: 488]

Rather than freeing children to form new attachments, a sense of having been abandoned probably increases children's emotional dependency on their parents. Workers have observed that "unvisited children seemed more attached to their parents than visited children," and continued to "pine" for parents who no longer visited them [Fanshel & Shinn 1978: 404]. This process is understandable, as "physical and emotional distancing promotes rather than weakens psychological dependency" [Laird 1979: 191]. Many children in care idealize their parents and fantasize about a reunion that will satisfy all their longings [Hinton 1978; Laird 1979]. Attempts to loosen a child's psychological ties by severing contact only perpetuates the child's idealization of his parents [Steinhauer 1991].

The persistence of attachment over time is shown when youths reach the age for leaving care and seek out their families:

in a group of foster care "graduates" (N=277), 83% had ongoing contact with their families [Festinger 1983]. The importance of extended family and siblings is illustrated by the pattern of these contacts. In the Festinger study, 48% of those leaving care had contacts with parents; the remaining 35% were in touch with extended family members. In a study by Jones and Moses [1984], 78% of young adults formerly in care said their siblings were a major resource for them. It is believed that many youths try to reestablish relationships with their families, even when they have not seen them in many years [Ryan et al. 1988].

Children need to know that their foster carers accept their family ties; otherwise they may feel that to be loyal to their parents they must distance themselves from their foster families. If forced to choose between families, the children may pick the lost family they have idealized and give up the carers who could still be an important part of their lives ["Taking Control" Project 1985]. This outcome may be avoided if regular family contact is part of the placement experience.

Need for Support after Discharge. The usual age for discharge from foster care is 18, an age when a great many young people are still receiving psychological and financial support from their families. At this writing, a momentum is building in the United States to prepare youths for independent living and to support their movement into it. Many youths leaving foster care, however, are still being set adrift to fend for themselves [Meston 1988; Raychaba 1993]; agency custody is simply terminated and the youths are expected to function as adults [Hardin 1988]. This differs starkly from the flexibility given to most young people, who come and go from their family homes as they test out their ability to live independently. A limited number of publicly funded programs are allowing agencies to provide extended support to adolescents being discharged from foster care, but available statistics suggest that at least 50% of those leaving care are not being covered by these programs [Allen et al. 1988]. Those youths not included are likely to be the most at risk of exclusion from society:

> Youths who are emotionally unstable or seriously delin-
> quent are usually not approved for subsidy programs,
> principally because of the risk of agency liability should a
> youth cause or suffer harm while in an independent-living
> placement. [Irvine 1988]

Graduates of foster care are likely to have more emotional problems than children who have grown up in their own families. The persistence of emotional problems was found in a longitudinal study of children in care: their behavior improved over time, but their emotional problems tended to persist [Palmer 1979]. Although respondents to some surveys have tended to express satisfaction with their experience in foster care [Rice & McFadden 1988], other studies show "a substantial proportion...surviving only marginally in a society with which they are unprepared to cope" [Festinger 1983]. A group of older adolescents invited to discuss their foster care experience in an agency meeting were described as

> full of rage and worry about themselves. They expressed
> deep feelings of inferiority and worthlessness and per
> ceived themselves as being treated as second-class citi
> zens. They hated the system that makes them different.
> [Rice & McFadden 1988]

Considering these problems, young people leaving care need some kind of family contact as a source of moral support and caring through their vulnerable late teen and early adult years. Yet, many of those discharged from substitute care have no support system to which they can turn [Allen et al. 1988]. Many adolescents do not form lasting attachments to their foster carers: they often move into these homes at a time when they are looking toward discharge and dealing with earlier conflicts that resurface at this stage of their development [Ryan et al. 1988]. Estimates of continuing contact of youths with foster carers vary. "For most young people leaving foster care, there is a definite break with their former foster families" [Ryan et al. 1988: 564], although Jones and Moses [1984] found that 51% of 328 youths in their first year of discharge had contact with their former foster families at least once a month.

The tendency for youths leaving care to reconnect with their biological families suggests that agencies should be protective of these ties. Child welfare professionals cannot assume that families who were unable or unwilling to care for children at a particular time will never be able to offer them support. An illustration of the persistence of family bonds was given by a Native Indian mother whose four children were placed in care, apparently because of her alcoholism ["Taking Control" Project 1982]. At a conference many years later, she reported that she had stopped drinking within a year of the placements, but was unsuccessful in her appeal to the government child welfare officials to have her children returned from foster care. She finally achieved reunion with her children after 16 years: when she knew the youngest child was old enough to be discharged from care, she placed an advertisement in the local newspaper. Her oldest daughter answered the advertisement three days after it appeared, and gradually connected her with the other children, two of whom came to live with her. It can be argued that family ties are particularly strong among Native Indian families, because of their cultural values and ties to their communities, or that the child welfare authorities may have underestimated the mother's strength, because of generally held beliefs about the chronicity of drinking problems among Native Indians. This case does show, however, the potential strength of family ties, both in the mother's persistence and in the speed with which her children achieved reunion with her.

A supportive program for youths leaving care reported success in repairing their relationships with parents, finding that

Even...where parent-child relationships are historically torn, scarred and strained, the youth often gravitates homeward out of a need to have contact with and receive support from blood-tie relationships. [Anderson & Simonitch 1981: 387–388]

Generally, research and practice emphasize the importance of family relationships during and after foster care. Like all human beings, adolescents moving toward independence need to feel that someone cares about them. We cannot assume that foster carers will be providing this kind of ongoing support. For this reason alone, we must do everything possible to maintain children's ties with their families.

Continuity in Care

Permanency Planning. The child's need for continuity is a major principle of placement. This principle has been conceptualized as *permanency planning*, "the process of taking prompt, decisive action to maintain children in their own homes or place them permanently with other families" [Maluccio & Fein 1983: 195]. It is well accepted, and supported by empirical evidence, that "parents are by far the most likely source of permanency for children" [Fanshel 1981: ix]. At the primary and secondary levels of planning, therefore, permanency is achieved by keeping children in their own homes or returning them to their homes as soon as possible after placement. At the tertiary level, it is achieved by providing a substitute home that lasts as long as the child requires it.

Placement in a Familiar Environment. Continuity can be provided for children by placing them with people they already know, such as relatives (kinship care), a practice that often takes place informally. Major concerns about such placements are the possibility of generalized family problems, and the hazards of negotiating boundaries with biological parents who may have free access to their children in the homes of friends or relatives

[Dubowitz et al. 1993]. A comparison of children in regular agency foster homes versus those in informal placements found no support for the concern that there would be a lower quality of care in the latter [Lewis & Fraser 1987].

Placement in a familiar home is consistent with informal placement practices: in 1990, almost half the children in foster care in Illinois and New York City were placed with relatives [Dubowitz et al. 1993]. It is also in line with the principle of continuity, as articulated in the Declaration of Principles in Ontario's Child and Family Services Act: "To recognize that the least restrictive or disruptive course of action that is available and is appropriate...should be followed" [Ontario 1984].

Empirical studies support the benefits of placements that are consistent with children's past experiences. Increased stability is found when children are placed with relatives [Berridge & Cleaver 1987], or with families of similar socioeconomic status [Parker 1966]. The postdischarge functioning of children placed with relatives compares favorably with that of other children in care: the former did better in school, had more contact with their families, and had fewer identity problems than the latter [Rowe et al. 1984]. In a study comparing children in all types of substitute care, those placed with relatives did best in terms of school functioning at four months postdischarge, and in terms of emotional and developmental functioning at six to ten months postdischarge [Fein et al. 1983].

The foregoing findings are not surprising: children who are placed in homes similar to their own should be less disoriented and better able to integrate their past and present experiences than those placed in unfamiliar settings. When placed with relatives, these children have the additional advantage of belonging to the same extended family, which minimizes culture shock and identity confusion.

Continuity of Workers. Social work principles emphasize the value of a trusting worker-client relationship. It is especially important for children in care to be able to trust their workers, given the power that workers have over their lives. The limited evidence available suggests that a child's initial worker is likely to be replaced, possibly many times. A study of 200 children in long-term care (at least three years) found that they experienced a mean of eight different workers over a mean of five years in care [Palmer 1976]. Some of these changes are created by worker turnover: a 1987 survey of frontline workers in Ontario CASs (N=787) showed that 53% stayed less than three years [Cantrell 1988]. Other changes are created by bureaucratic structures.

Agency structures often create discontinuity for children by assigning workers according to the child's status (e.g., at home, in temporary care, eligible for adoption), or attaching workers to particular foster homes. Thus, the children lose their worker when they undergo a change in their status or their placement. Empirically, a correlation between worker change and placement change was found in a large study of 4,288 children in foster care [Pardeck 1984: 507].

In summary, the best way to provide continuity for children is by maintaining them in or reunifying them with their own families. For children who must be in care, placements with friends or relatives provide continuity; the latter provide additional benefits. Continuity of workers is also an issue, and agency structures that create discontinuity should be reviewed from this perspective.

Openness from Workers and Caregivers

Acknowledgment of Discontinuity. Many youths in care have unresolved inner problems arising from personal histories of abandonment and/or unpredictable separation [Fahlberg 1985]. They need some validation from workers and caregivers that their placement experiences have been disruptive and difficult for them. The young adults in Festinger's postdischarge study [1983] looked back on their changes of home as unsettling and confusing. Moreover, their scores on satisfaction with foster care were inversely correlated with the number of moves they experienced [1983].

Some types of moves are viewed as desirable by workers, for example, a move from a group home to family foster care, or from family foster care to adoption, but for children, even such desirable moves may be experienced as a time of loss. Looking back nine years at her move from a group home to a foster home, one young woman said:

> even thinking about it now brings a lump to my throat, but at the time I cried, like a dog does in the throat, and I didn't want [my foster carers] to see. I didn't want them to feel that I was ungrateful, but really, with all my heart I wished I wasn't going. [Kahan 1979: 104]

Children's aversion to moving is shown by their concern about the moves of other children in the same home. An adult previously in care recalled:

> Freddie…came [to the foster home] first of all with me. I don't remember what happened to Freddie, he was there one day, and he wasn't the next. Where he went to I've no idea, I didn't even know he was going. [Kahan 1979: 103]

The persistence of this childhood memory illustrates the stress of living with the unexplained arrivals and departures of other children, especially when one's own status is not secure.

Information about the Past. Children's awareness of their family backgrounds and why they are in care are important aspects of self-knowledge, and the latter has been identified as contributing to good adjustment [Thorpe 1974] and to placement success [Holman 1974]. Research with adults has shown that the events of their childhood were less important to them than their ability to come to terms with those events [Main et al. 1985]. It was important for these adults to remember their early experiences, and to understand and forgive their parents for behavior about which they had negative memories.

A psychiatrist working with children in treatment foster homes noted that they wanted information from their families, even though it was upsetting to learn about family problems. Those who received no information appeared to interpret "no news" as "bad news" [Fine 1985]. Moreover, children who lack knowledge of their own backgrounds are at a disadvantage when questioned by their peers. Two boys in care said they were taunted about not having a "mum," and a girl reported feeling embarrassed and different from other children [NFCA 1988].

Despite widespread recognition that children need information about their backgrounds, they commonly have unanswered questions, even after many years in care [Beste & Richardson 1981]. When children in long-term care were asked about their parents, over one-fourth had no information about their mothers, and only one-third had three or more items of information [Rowe et al. 1984]. They expressed curiosity about their families, but had difficulty asking questions about them.

A study of children's case records found little mention of any clinical work to help them come to terms with their family relationships [Fanshel et al. 1989]. Adolescents in foster care, meeting formally to discuss their experiences, have mentioned the lack of preparation they received when entering agency care [OACAS 1988]. They would have liked clear arrangements for family visiting, and placements closer to home to reduce alienation from their families, friends, and communities.

Workers may withhold information from children to protect them from knowledge that may be painful; in the process, however, they leave children to develop their own accounts. Often, children imagine the worst. As one child said, "The only reason that I can think of for my mother not to want me is if there is something terribly wrong with me or terribly wrong with her. Either way, I've had it" [Geiser 1973: 35]. Another expressed a similar feeling—that there was something wrong with him—to his worker: "I wish I could die and be born again as a *proper* child"; when questioned, he was found to be referring to his foster status [Ville Marie Social Services 1989].

In summary, many children have gaps in knowledge and unanswered questions about the past, suggesting that workers may be purposely withholding information from them. Children need to know about their backgrounds and their families, to help them accept being in care, and to keep them from making negative inferences about themselves.

Biological Families: Potential for Continued Parenting

In the early days of child welfare, little attention was given to supporting at-risk families so that they might keep their children at home, but child welfare practice now recognizes that children's families represent their best chance for achieving permanence [Gibson & Noble 1991]. Programs to prevent placement, to keep parents involved with their children in care, and to provide follow-up help to maintain children who have been returned to their own homes are being developed and implemented, but encounter many difficulties, as described below.

Prevention of Placement

Environmental Stress on Families. Many families whose children are placed in foster care are under constant stress because they are poor: low income is the best predictor of a child's removal from home [Lindsey 1991]. Because they are poor, these families are also likely to be subject to other debilitating conditions, such as residence in a high-problem neighborhood, single parenthood, and inadequate nutrition. Many of the families whose children enter care have experienced exclusion and discrimination from the wider community because they are visible minorities: children from families of color and Native Indian families tend to be overrepresented in care [Close 1983; Mannes 1993]. Generally, families whose children enter care have been excluded from mainstream society: a study of families who neglected their children found they scored high on scales of social alienation, had low participation in social organizations, and had weak support systems [Polansky et al. 1981].

Families who are overwhelmed by the stress of poverty and alienated from mainstream society may consequently fail to provide adequate child care, or they may request placement of their children as a survival strategy. Attempts to prevent placement must take account of all these conditions. It is not a simple matter of motivating parents to work harder to care for their children; somehow, their environment must be strengthened to provide reinforcement for them as a family.

In working with families beset by destructive environments, it is important for practitioners to identify family strengths: the assumption must be that "families are good for, rather than bad for, children," that they are "competent but constrained instead of incompetent and pathological" [Cimmarusti 1992: 244]. Some programs are addressing the constraints on families by going into their homes and offering concrete help, including training in parenting skills [Walton et al. 1993]. Ideally, intervention should go beyond the immediate family, to the extended family, the community, and all relevant systems that impinge on a child's welfare [Cimmarusti 1992].

Intensive Family Preservation Services (IFPS). Intensive family preservation programs provide home-based, short-term, highly concentrated crisis intervention services for families in imminent danger of child placement. Casework skills of a high order are necessary to use the emotional intensities of the crisis to bring about rapid change [Kinney et al. 1990; Pecora et al. 1992]. Other kinds of family preservation services that are not operating under crisis conditions, such as family reunification, often use some features of IFPS.

Handling Demands to Place Adolescents. An increasing

number of families have been requesting agency placement because they are overwhelmed by the demands of parenting difficult adolescents [MacDonald 1992]. Such placements are likely to be short-term solutions at best; intervention is more likely to be effective when addressed to an intact family [Balbernie 1974]. As most parent-adolescent conflicts arise from autonomy struggles or family enmeshment, the adolescent's individuation is more likely to be achieved successfully through the family's joint exploration of the members' interdependent, guilt-laden obligations rather than through abrupt separation [Boszormenyi-Nagy 1973]. Family therapy has proved to be a successful response to adolescents who are challenging authority: one program aimed at status offenders reduced the percentage who had to be placed from 44% to 4% over a two-year period [Michaels & Green 1979].

To engage parents in counseling when they are demanding placement, agencies must find a way of containing their sense of imminent crisis. One program uses an innovative approach by agreeing to placement while insisting that families engage in several planning sessions toward that end [MacDonald 1992]. As the parents consider the family dynamics that have led to the request for placement, and the long-term future implications of family breakup, they agree to delay placement while they engage in further counseling toward the goal of maintaining the family.

Another approach to placement prevention is to reduce the stress on families by involving the adolescents in afterschool programs, combining lifeskills training with recreation during the high-risk hours of the day [Hamilton-Wentworth 1990]. These programs are supplemented by groupwork with parents to discuss the handling of adolescent behavior problems.

Generally, the child welfare field has broadened its range of responses to families-at-risk, and is investing additional resources in structured programs to keep children in their own homes. It is important that these responses move beyond the level of demonstration programs in progressive agencies and become established in child welfare practice as a whole.

Modified Care Programs

The traditional approach to foster care has been to move children totally away from their families to a substitute home or environment. Even when plans involve early reunification of children with their families, it is natural for the worker's time and resources to shift to the home where the children are currently living. As there is usually little connection between the parental home and the foster home, children have no sense of continuity [Fein & Maluccio 1992].

Continuity can be maintained for children by the use of modified care arrangements. Modified care is based on the principle of relieving parents temporarily of part of their child-caring responsibility, and concurrently helping them to improve their ability to care for their children. It also aims to minimize the traumatic effects of separation.

Modified care has a variety of forms: foster day care, short-term placement with neighbors, placement on weekends only, placement during the week with return home on weekends and/or holidays, and periodic short-term placement to help parents through critical periods. Foster day care seems to have been used mainly for younger children, who eat all their meals and go to school from the foster home, but return to their parents at night [Pavelson 1972]. It could, however, be used with adolescents to avoid identity problems and rifts in family relationships that result from traditional foster care placements. Short-term placement with neighbors has been used to avoid the disrupting effects of placing children in a completely new environment [Barr 1971]. A program in Cleveland, Ohio, provided foster care for children during the week on a short-term basis (less than one year), while they continued to live with their parents on weekends and holidays [Loewe & Hanrahan 1975]. Social workers help the children and parents to establish relationships with the foster carers and to improve their relationships with each other.

The traditional pattern of having children live in foster care and see their families on weekends has been reversed by some programs [Astrachan & Harris 1983]. This may be particularly effective for parents who are substance abusers, or for adolescents whose behavior tends to worsen on weekends. A program in Leeds, England, brought young male offenders into residential treatment on weekends only; they remained in their own homes during the week and were given intensive casework together with their families [Balbernie 1974]. Yet another approach is to have foster carers take children for periodic short-term crisis relief, when the parental home is marginally adequate [Gabinet 1983]. In these latter models, the foster carer is clearly a support—not a replacement—for the parents, who retain their roles and responsibilities.

Family Reactions to Placement

Families whose children enter care often live in nonsupportive environments and have been marginalized by society. As a result, they are likely to feel alienated from society and antagonistic toward authority figures, including the workers who handle placement of their children. The loss of their children is likely to increase their sense of inadequacy, powerlessness, and societal stigmatization [Steinhauer 1991].

Parents' feelings about placement have received too little attention from researchers. One study found that mothers who were identified as neglecting or abusing their children were angry at the agency: a cluster analysis identified a group who viewed the agency as a "usurper" of child care and parental rights [Jenkins & Norman 1975]. Mothers from the lowest socioeconomic group in this study viewed the agency as aggravating their problems, and felt that their workers were disinterested and unhelpful.

Underlying this parental anger are feelings of failure, despondency, and guilt about having their children in foster care [Jenkins & Norman 1975; Lee & Nisivoccia 1989]. A biological mother described a range of painful feelings, including her sense that the foster carer's positive remarks about how well her children were doing were "an implied criticism of the care I had given my child" [McAdams 1972].

Parents may be afraid to work toward their children's return, for fear they might fail again [Jenson & Whittaker 1987]. In particular, they may be discouraged by the socioeconomic gap between themselves and the foster carers, feeling that they cannot offer their children the opportunities they have in the placement [Jenson & Whittaker 1987].

Feelings of anger and discouragement may not be expressed openly, but rather transformed into passive resistance toward workers and foster carers. Passivity is probably the most common reaction to placement: parents withdraw from the agency, and thereby, from contact with their children [McAdams 1972; "Taking Control" Project 1985]. It is understandable that parents may be reluctant to visit their children: the foster carers are strangers, who may disapprove of them; the most tangible aspects of their role as parents have been lost; and they have few guidelines for the "visiting" relationship [Millham et al. 1986]. Parents who do visit may express their alienation in inappropriate behaviors that discourage workers from planning further visits [Fanshel 1982].

Workers must find ways to counteract the tendency for parents to resist constructive involvement with the agency [Lee & Nisivoccia 1989]. Otherwise, parents may fail to follow-up on referrals that might help them to attain resources needed for family reunification [Lee & Nisivoccia 1989]. Workers and foster carers can be influential in encouraging or discouraging ongoing family ties. Parents may feel diminished by comments from workers or foster carers that reflect on them as parents: even reassurances that their children are happy may be interpreted as unfavorable comparisons of the parental home with the foster home [McAdams 1972]. "Intervening in families must be done with great care to avoid actions which could weaken the natural family system, sap its vitality and strength, or force it to make difficult, costly adjustments" [Laird 1979: 177].

The development of mutual support groups is one positive response to parents with children [Jenson & Whittaker 1987]. The opportunity to share experiences with others is particularly important for families who find it difficult to talk openly with workers because they are alienated by the workers' authority. Meeting with other parents of children in care provides parents with an outlet for their strong feelings and can be a source of support for their efforts toward reunification with their children.

Desire for Continuing Responsibility

When children are admitted to agency care, their parents are often "completely displaced in their children's lives by agency staff and foster parents" [Blumenthal 1984: 4]. Yet parents do not expect agencies to assume almost total responsibility for their children: they have expressed shock and dismay that this occurs [Millham et al. 1986]. In particular, parents reported feeling betrayed when they requested agency help, and social workers then used compulsion to have their parental rights set aside.

Packman and colleagues' study of parents' perceptions indicated that many felt unwanted by agencies and foster carers: if their children had been taken into care compulsorily, they had a sense of being pushed aside and losing their parental responsibilities [Packman et al. 1986]. In this study of 75 parents who objected to their children's placement, 90% said they were not told where their children were being taken, and "hardly any parents accompanied their children into care" [Packman et al. 1986: 134].

Workers tend to underestimate parents' sense of responsibility for their children in care [Berridge & Cleaver 1987]. Researchers noted that some families affirmed a permanent commitment to their children, yet their social workers

> consistently underrated the amount of continued responsibility and concern they felt for their children, tending to interpret relief as rejection and to give insufficient recognition to the value of continued contact between parents and children. [Fisher et al. 1986: 72]

Workers often draw conclusions about parents' commitment to their children from their visiting patterns. As noted above, there are many conditions of placement that influence parents to withdraw from contact, yet workers tend to discount these reasons and interpret the parents' behavior as rejection of their child [Fisher et al. 1986]. As a result, the workers may fail to encourage parents to keep in touch with their children. Considering the parents' vulnerability, "social workers and foster parents need to make extraordinary efforts to encourage parents to visit" [NFCA 1987]. Parents who were encouraged to participate in a structured visiting program expressed their concern about their capacity to provide a healthy family life for their children [Simms & Bolden 1991]. They used the opportunity to meet other parents of children in care and expressed their desire to improve their ability to care for their children.

Contact as a Key to Success

There is little information in the literature about the frequency of family visits with their children in care, but indications are that many children are not visited. A survey of 70 preschool children in care showed that 37% were not being actively visited by their parents [Simms & Bolden 1991]. Agency resources are often insufficient to support visiting, which can be complicated and time consuming: consequently, visiting plans that require support are often allowed to lapse [Hess et al. 1992].

Visiting is a vital part of any placement program. The philosophy of permanency planning requires that parental contact be encouraged, as the family is viewed as the best resource for providing permanency to children. Parents' cooperation in maintaining contact with their children is used as a test of their interest; their performance is an important consideration when a court decides whether to terminate parental rights and free children for a permanent substitute home. Moreover, the value of ongoing family contact for children in care has been demonstrated in terms of better adjustment in care, earlier reunion, and successful discharge.

Adjustment of Children. A number of studies have linked parental visiting of children with better progress in out-of-home care. Children who were visited, when compared to those who were not, had higher "average well-being" [Weinstein 1960], better "adjustment to residential care" [Petrie 1962], and were more likely to be diagnosed as "not disturbed" [Eisenberg 1962; Jenkins 1969]. The visited children also had less soiling and ill-health [Holman 1973]; a more "adequate" conception of foster status [Thorpe 1974]; better functioning [Fanshel & Shinn 1978]; better behavior in a correctional institution [Borgman 1985]; higher ratings on psychological, social, and educational measures [Millham et al. 1986]; and a higher success rate in completing a residential treatment program [Savas et al. 1993].

Visiting has been linked with positive attitudes on the part of both the biological families and the foster carers. Frequent contact was associated with improvement in parental feelings toward placement [Jenkins & Norman 1972] and with positive attitudes on the part of foster carers toward families [Palmer 1983a]. Furthermore, foster carers who supported contact were able to help children "work through feelings about [biological] family problems and to minimize feelings of marginality, isolation and deviance" [Fine 1985]. Possibly, the regularity of visiting is more important than its frequency. The limited available research suggests that children's difficulties are more likely to be linked with infrequent visiting than with no contact at all [Jenkins 1969; Holman 1973].

Overall, most empirical findings support family contact as beneficial to children's adjustment. The issues of infrequent visiting and the influence of foster family attitudes need further exploration.

Early Reunion. Current research indicates that children who have family contact during placement are more likely to return home [Levitt 1981; Lawder et al. 1986; Simms & Bolden 1991], and their return home is likely to take place earlier [Mech 1985; Millham et al. 1986] than those who lack such contact. As Steinhauer [1991] states, visiting is a means of ensuring that a temporary placement is not allowed, by neglect, to develop into a permanent one.

Postdischarge Outcomes. Postdischarge outcomes tend to be better when children have kept in touch with their families, either by ongoing contact or temporary reunions. The postdischarge functioning of children who had been temporarily reunited with their families during placement was better than that of children who remained continuously in care: the former group had better family adjustment, emotional and developmental functioning, and school functioning [Fein et al. 1983]. Moreover, temporary reunion was the variable most strongly associated with positive outcomes among the many child, family, and casework variables examined in this study.

The likelihood of recidivism, in the sense of return to foster care, was lessened when children had family contact during placement [Block 1981], when the family and child had been previously reunited, or when the placement had been with relatives [Fein et al. 1983]. The quality of reunion was also associated with visiting: children who had contact with their families during placement felt closer to them after reunion than those who did not [Festinger 1983]. Furthermore, children who had frequent contact early in the placement were more likely to feel "very close" to families at discharge than those who had less early contact [Festinger 1983].

The foregoing findings are understandable: visiting reassures children of their parents' affection, allows them to question their parents about the reason for placement, and probably minimizes discrepancies in the explanations that children receive from their parents, workers, and foster carers. All these influences are likely to reduce the children's sense of being rejected or abandoned, easing their reincorporation back into their homes and families.

Help to Families during and after Placement

The intensive family preservation services mentioned above are preventive services addressed to families whose children are still at home. Families also need support after their children are placed, first to improve conditions so that their children can be returned, and then to maintain these improvements.

The permanency planning movement of the early 1980s initially reduced the number of children in care, probably because agencies were oriented toward avoiding placement, involving families in the placement process, and working toward earlier reunification [Fein & Maluccio 1992]. By the end of the 1980s, however, reentry rates began to rise, a trend that has been linked with lack of maintenance work with families after reunification [Fein & Maluccio 1992]. For example, a study of 100 families reunited with their children found that 24 showed no reported improvement in the parental problems that led to their children's removal [Turner 1984].

Demonstration programs have shown that families who are given intensive help after their children are placed are more likely to be reunited with their children [Boyd 1979; Jones 1985; Fein & Staff 1991; Walton et al. 1993]; moreover, support to families after reunification appeared to prevent reentry into care [Lahti et al. 1978; Turner 1984; Jones 1985]. Most families, however, receive services for less than six months after their children return home [Fein & Maluccio 1992, citing Barth & Berry 1990].

Family reunification services are especially important when adolescents have been placed because their families viewed the youths as beyond their control. The proportion of adolescents in care increased rapidly in the 1980s, and first placements were usually attributed to behavioral or relationship problems [Fein & Maluccio 1992]. A Canadian study of 163 children and adolescents admitted to care in the previous six months indicated that 49% were there primarily because their parents could not handle their behavior [Palmer 1983a].

Reunion is more likely to be successful if workers have dealt with the troubled relationships between these adolescents and their families during the placement. If no effort is made to resolve differences, families will tend to reorganize without the placed adolescent, and negative feelings may become entrenched. This risk may be reduced by conjoint family treatment with parents, children, and possibly, the foster carers [Tiddy 1986]. If the foster carers are able to deal with the adolescent, they can help the family transfer these gains to their own home [Jenson & Whittaker 1987].

In summary, many children are in care because their families live in stressful conditions. Intensive family preservation programs support families in coping with these conditions, and have achieved a reduction in placements. Modified placement plans can help to maintain the integrity of the family, while protecting children. Many parents feel alienated from society and from the agencies that take over custody of their children. In order to keep parents involved with their children, and engage them in working toward reunification, these feelings must be addressed. Some success has been achieved by having parents join mutual support groups. Agencies must encourage—even insist—that parents visit regularly, and must engage them in working on the problems that led to placement.

Foster Carers: Limitations and Strengths in the Fostering Relationship

Foster care is usually provided by altruistic, family-oriented people who open their homes to children and adolescents in need. Foster care is limited, however, by its exclusion of families, by discontinuities in placement, and by the limited capacity of children to attach themselves to a new family. Its strengths and potential lie in the changing attitudes of foster carers, who increasingly view themselves as providing special treatment to children rather than replacing their families.

Excluding Parents from Foster Care

The historical development of foster care has left a legacy of possessiveness on the part of foster carers. An early form of care for dependent children was apprenticeship, which bound children to their masters. By the twentieth century, local governments paid foster carers a small subsidy for expenses, but older children were expected to work for their board, in farm labor, housework, or child care. With increasing affluence and emphasis on education, society came to expect less work of children in families generally; accordingly, rates paid to foster carers were increased to cover, at least in part, the expenses they incurred. Old assumptions that children in care owe tangible compensation to their caregivers no longer exist. Nevertheless, foster carers share their homes and volunteer their time, so it is natural for them to expect some return. The most natural compensation is for the placed child to form an attachment to the foster carers; the foster carers may view this as incompatible with the child's having strong family attachments.

"Exclusive" fostering is defined as favoring containment of children within the foster family and excluding them from other connections [Holman 1974]. Three empirical studies found that 50% to 63% of foster carers regarded the children "as their own," and 35% to 56% thought that biological parents should not be encouraged to visit their children in care [Holman 1974]. A study of 92 foster mothers found that 33% had an exclusive orientation, that is, they "rejected the fostering role," and a further 15% were unsure or did not enjoy thinking of themselves as "foster" parents [Adamson 1973: 161].

Exclusive foster carers tend to measure their success by the degree to which they can replace the child's family: they often vigorously oppose family visiting, claiming that it upsets the child [Steinhauer 1991]. Even if their dislike of visits is not made explicit, foster carers may convey enough of their attitude subverbally that children, in order to placate them, hide their interest in having family contact [Ryan et al. 1981; Berridge & Cleaver 1987]. It is difficult for workers to deal with foster carers who are opposed to visiting, because that opposition may be denied, externalized, or projected onto others [Wald et al. 1988].

An exclusive approach makes it difficult for children to integrate their past and present lives. Exclusive foster carers tend to deny the importance of the child's past, wishing to emphasize the present [Holman 1974]. Social work visits, parental contact, or children's questions about their "other" lives represent a threat, because they contradict the accepted view in the home, i.e., that the child is part of the foster family [Holman 1974].

Although exclusive fostering is contraindicated by theory and practice principles, it tends to persist. "A high degree of tension and competitiveness often exists" between parents and foster carers, causing the latter to discourage contact [Cautley 1980]. Many foster mothers "acknowledge a need to be loved and appreciated by their foster children" [Steinhauer 1991: 160]. Viewing children's families as their rivals for children's affection, they may attempt to undermine family attachments [Steinhauer 1991].

Discontinuity in Placement

Prevalence of Serial Placements. Statistics on placement changes are difficult to compare, because differing approaches to reporting are used, but it is clear that many children experience serial placements. During a median time of two and one-half years in care, 22% of 4,288 children in one study had three or more placements [Pardeck 1984]; after two years in care, 56% of 170 children studied had three or more placements [Millham et al. 1986]; during a median time of four years in care, 48% of 73 children studied had three or more placements [Kufeldt et al. 1989]; and a study of all children in "permanent" care in Ontario showed they averaged three placements during an average of five years in care [Crown Ward Administrative Review 1991]. Furthermore, several studies have identified subgroups of children who experienced an unconscionable number of moves: 14% of 170 children had five or more [Millham et al. 1986]; 18% of 73 children had six or more [Kufeldt et al. 1989]; and 26% of 161 children had four or more different homes [Packman et al. 1986].

Moving children from one foster home to another is so characteristic of the foster care system that researchers have defined the experience of children as "stable" if they have had only two different foster homes [Pardeck 1984]. Moves may even be built into the system: many agencies include an initial temporary placement as part of their placement planning. From a child's viewpoint, however, the experience of trying to adapt to a new family, then having to move again, can be disruptive. Certainly, children exposed to a series of placements cannot possibly feel secure when, as expressed by an adult previously in care, "all they want is somebody who really cares" [Kahan 1979: 112]. Given the difficulty of ensuring for children a single, stable, continuous environment in care, foster carers should be encouraged to accept children's families as part of their lives: "Parental and wider family links, however unsuitable they may seem on other grounds, may be the only enduring relationship the child enjoys" [Millham et al. 1986: 116].

Reasons for Breakdown. Placement breakdown has been associated with children's behaviors such as failing to attach, running away, and being passive-aggressive [Walsh & Walsh 1990], and with behavioral and emotional problems [Pardeck 1984].

Other reasons for placement breakdown are only indirectly related to the child. When foster carers are given adequate pay, training, and support, it seems they can handle difficult children for as long as placement is necessary [Levin et al. 1976; Meadowcroft & Trout 1990]. Reasons given by foster carers who drop out of the system include lack of training and support from agencies, as well as the increasing severity of problems presented by the children placed with them [Chamberlain et al. 1992]. The author's informal discussions with foster carers over the years have revealed that they often feel that children are "dumped" on them with little preparation and little information about the child's background. It may be that the workers themselves have little information about a child; or they may be tempted to minimize problems, fearing that the foster carer might decline to take the child.

The uncertainty of a child's future creates further difficulties for regular foster carers. It is difficult to predict how long a child will need care, as this will depend on the family's motivation and capacity. This uncertainty is likely to undermine the commitment of foster carers: they can neither look forward to being relieved of a difficult child after a definite number of months nor can they risk making a strong commitment to a child who may be moved at any time. Under these circumstances, they are unlikely to give priority to the needs of a child whose behavior disrupts their family's life.

Foster carers face many pitfalls in their work with children, such as behavior problems that are rooted in the child's past and aggravated by the developmental crises of adolescence. Foster carers also face the stress of working with limited information, modest compensation, and insufficient support.

Children's Limited Ability to Relate to Caregivers

Children who have been separated from their parents are likely to maintain an emotional distance from their foster carers. They are likely to be fearful of another rejection, confused about family loyalties, and resentful about the loss of control over their own lives.

Fear of Rejection. After the trauma of having to leave a familiar home and family, children are likely to be sensitive to any indication of rejection by caregivers. An older boy in care recalled crying uncontrollably when his foster mother left him temporarily in a train station [NFCA 1988]. Another teenage boy said, "You need about half a year to find out if they care or if they're bothered about you" [NFCA 1988]. Two adults previously in care revealed their vivid and painful memories of many years earlier, when they had been locked out by their foster carers because they missed their curfews [Kahan 1979].

Most placement plans are somewhat indefinite because they depend upon events within the child's family; the resulting uncertainty is likely to be stressful for children. It would probably ease children's anxieties if this uncertainty was discussed with them and they were reassured that workers and foster carers would share all relevant information with them. In the author's experience, workers and caregivers tend to discuss placement plans with children as though each new home will be available for as long as they need it. When they see other children being moved, and particularly when they themselves are moved, children may well begin to feel like pawns in a game whose rules they don't understand. An adult formerly in care described alternative care systems for children as paternalistic, controlling, and disempowering [Raychaba 1993].

Children's reluctance to make an emotional commitment to their foster carers is illustrated by two brothers who experienced seven successive placements:

> When someone new [foster carers] came along, we thought it would be the same old story. They would foster us for two months, then take us back...we thought we would be having to do that until we were sixteen. [Kahan 1979]

It is understandable that children will guard against opening themselves to a new family, when their experience indicates that they can expect to be rejected again. Fearful of the pain that follows from broken attachments, children may try to avoid attachment altogether, often through disruptive behavior [Raychaba 1993]. This increases the chance of placement breakdown, as foster carers become frustrated with the child's difficult behavior and lack of emotional responsiveness [Wilkes 1992]. Empirical research shows that placement breakdown is associated with a high number of previous placements [Walsh & Walsh 1990].

Conflicts about Family Loyalties. The tensions created by placement may lead to "a triangulated conflict among parents, children, and foster parents" [Meyer 1984: 499]. In particular, children are likely to experience strong loyalty conflicts when their families are hostile to their foster carers [Fine 1985]. Many children in care are "trapped in the memories of an earlier family, and lack the means to resolve their pain. Thus, although they may live in a new family, they lack the freedom to join it" [Campbell 1991]. These observations were supported by a quantitative analysis demonstrating greater placement stability for children whose foster carers had positive attitudes toward their parents [Palmer 1983a].

A child's difficulty in maintaining ties with two families during placement is suggested by a postdischarge study comparing 277 graduates from group and foster care: 88% of 118 group home graduates were in contact with their families, compared to only 49% of 276 children from foster homes [Festinger 1983]. Further, group home graduates were more likely than foster home graduates to report feeling "very close" to their families [Festinger 1983: 177–8]. This pattern is consistent with the observation that children "may shun contact with the natural parents in order to avoid upsetting or antagonizing [the foster carers]" [Steinhauer 1991: 160].

The custom of using parental titles for foster carers probably contributes to children's sense of divided loyalties. An adult formerly in care recalled, "for somebody to say 'Well, I'm not your Auntie Elspeth anymore, I'm Mum now, you can call me Mum!'...I didn't like that" [Kahan 1979: 106]. The British National Foster Care Association has attempted to reduce confusion for children by changing its terminology from *foster parent* to *foster carer*; it suggests that children may feel disloyal to their parents if they establish a close relationship with foster carers, and "the use of the term foster parent can exacerbate this problem" [Lowe 1991: 154].

In summary, children's past rejections and conflicting loyalties limit their ability to form attachments to foster carers. It is important that foster carers recognize this as a pattern unrelated to their personal characteristics and efforts, and do not have unrealistic expectations of children becoming part of their family.

Anger Projected on Caregivers. As noted above, children subjected to moves may resent the adults who seem to be controlling the major decisions of their lives. Underlying this resentment may be disappointment with parents who are not caring for them, but children may need to idealize their families and therefore displace their feelings onto their relationships with workers and foster carers [Tiddy 1986]. The destructive behavior of many children in foster care can be viewed as an expression of the distrust, anxiety, and rage they feel toward adults generally [Steinhauer 1974]. "Emotional and behavioral problems resulting from past histories of family violence often manifest themselves in antisocial, hostile, and aggressive acting out behaviors" [Raychaba 1993].

Foster carers have the unenviable role of dealing with the fallout from unresolved pain from the child's past experiences. It is understandable that foster carers may feel harassed and unappreciated, which weakens their commitment to offering their home indefinitely. The form of children's destructive acts may be especially upsetting to foster carers, because the children's behavior often reflects the few facts and the fantasies they have about their lost parents [Laird 1979].

> Barbara, a Native Indian girl who was adopted by a Caucasian family, was apparently a model "daughter" until age 15. Then she began to drink and become involved in casual sex, in keeping with her memories of her older sister's behavior. Her adoptive parents could not cope with Barbara's behavior; at 17 she was admitted to a psychiatric hospital, and the adoptive parents were unwilling to have her return to them.

The author worked with Barbara during her four-month stay in the psychiatric hospital, and discussed her memories of the frightening events in her family that led to her admission to care at age three. In Barbara's memory, no one had ever tried to discuss her past, which included witnessing her sister murder an abusive boyfriend. After discharge from the hospital, Barbara moved into a community group home and returned to school; when seen a year later, she appeared to have stopped acting out her past family experiences, and was doing well.

Professionals who work directly with placed children confirm the need of these children to remember their pasts. They emphasize that "the painful experiences of the past could not be left to sink into the unconscious to fester and cause later problems...but must be brought out into the open and dealt with" [Fitzgerald 1982: 42]. "Paradoxically, dealing with the biological family can promote more settling into the foster family" [Tiddy 1986: 56]. Foster carers require support from workers in helping children deal with the past, otherwise, their persistent pain may be expressed in ways that will lead to placement breakdown.

Need for Lowered Expectations. Considering the difficulty children have forming attachments to a new family, workers as well as foster carers are subjecting them to undue stress by having this expectation. An adult looking back on her move from a group home to a foster home felt that her foster carers were disappointed in her lack of response to them:

> It was a sort of whiney feeling in my throat and I didn't want to express myself in any way and I was like that for quite a few weeks after I arrived…I knew there was a wall being built up and even then…I think they made reports that I wasn't easy to get on with because they told me this. [Kahan 1979]

Other comments by children in care suggest that they feel similar pressures to meet the foster carers' expectation of emotional commitment. A teenage girl wrote, "It's hard to love your foster parents as much as you'd like to because you can't accept the fact that they are trying to be your stand-in parents and can't be your real parents no matter how hard they try" [OACAS 1971: 15]. Another girl in care said foster carers should not "expect too much too quickly…some children never accept foster parents, no matter how good they are to the children" [NFCA 1988]. A third young woman, age 20, had been deserted at age eight by her mother and spent six years in one foster home, yet she commented:

> Well, I don't think…I'd have been blissfully happy with anybody because I can remember my mother so vividly and anybody who deliberately steps out to take her place or gives me that impression immediately turns on a feeling of hate automatically. [Kahan 1979: 106]

Foster carers have also revealed their disappointment in children who are relatively unresponsive to them. At times of family stress, "Many foster parents either state directly that they are tired of constantly giving while getting nothing in return, or demonstrate their neediness behaviorally through an increased frustration with the foster child's inability to respond" [Steinhauer 1991: 160].

The desire to protect a child from pain may also influence foster carers and workers toward excluding biological families. A foster carer, commenting on the social work goal of keeping children in touch with both families, said she really agreed, "but it is agony to see *your* children being hurt by this constant reminder of the past" [Timms 1973] (emphasis added). As a result, "We have often encouraged children to estrange themselves from and to repress painful family experiences" [Laird 1979: 187]. This was exemplified vividly with Charlene, the five-year-old who saw both her parents killed by a car accident in which she was unhurt [Steinhauer 1991]. The foster carers showered her with attention and affection, but no one talked with her about the loss of her parents until she was brought to play therapy because she showed fear when riding in the family car.

Ideally, there should be a moratorium on expectations for children to attach themselves to foster carers. They should be free to maintain some emotional distance, moving gradually into the new relationship if and when they are able to develop an account of the past and a relationship with their families that they can accept.

Strengths and Potential Strengths in Fostering

Changes in Fostering. Child welfare practice is moving away from the traditional pattern in which workers act as mediators between foster carers and children's families, discouraging them from direct communication. One progressive influence has been the trend toward placing children with special needs in so-termed treatment foster homes, where the caregivers undertake a paraprofessional role [Meadowcroft & Trout 1990]. The treatment foster care model encourages family involvement on the part of foster carers, for example, by having them demonstrate the handling of behavioral difficulties and take a supportive role with parents [Meadowcroft & Trout 1990].

Changes in roles are also evident in regular foster care.

Foster carer competency is being upgraded, as more foster carers are being trained in behavior management skills, thus increasing their ability to accept and cope with difficult children [Titterington 1990]. Improved training and high expectations of foster carers include the recognition that they should be compensated for their skills, knowledge, and ability, and be accepted as members of the treatment team [Woolf 1990; Chamberlain et al. 1992].

These changes have moved foster carers in the direction of additional involvement with the families of the children in their care: they frequently assume responsibility for supervising visits, dealing with any complications that arise, and providing emotional support to both parents and children [Steinhauer 1984]. It has been suggested for some years that "if foster families are viewed as part of a professional team...intensive work with families would be possible and the foster family could serve as a valuable casework resource" [Maluccio & Sinanoglu 1981]. Steinhauer recommends that foster carers be treated "more as surrogate therapists and colleagues than as parent surrogates and clients" [Steinhauer 1991: 187].

Although regular foster care is still dependent on unpaid work by foster carers, the foregoing perspectives and trends have helped to reduce the possessiveness that characterized traditional fostering. As they move toward a paraprofessional role, foster carers are likely to be less competitive with children's families, and more willing to include those families in their children's lives.

Children's Ability to Relate to Two Families. The tendency of children in placement to experience divided loyalties may be aggravated by an "exclusive" orientation on the part of workers and foster carers. We know that children of divorcing parents can be loyal to both, if the parents permit. Research with young people leaving care shows that they can relate to both families when they are no longer dependent on agency care: in Festinger's study, 89% of 277 respondents continued to be in contact with their foster carers, and 83% were in contact with their families [1983]. In a similar vein, an experienced foster care worker in Kent (England) described to the author a pattern she had observed with young people who were eager to return to their families after leaving long-term care. Initially, they appeared to abandon their loyalties to foster carers, but eventually they were able to incorporate both relationships into their lives [Ralphs 1991]. These findings and observations support the concept of inclusive fostering, discussed below.

Open Recognition of Limits to Commitment. The following discussion draws on adoption theory, on the basis of its applicability to foster care. Adoption theory emphasizes the aspect of loss connected with adoption, i.e., that adoptees have at some point been abandoned by their biological families [Kirk 1984], which is also true for children in foster care. Kirk recommends that adoptive parents deal with children's loss by acknowledging the difference between biological and adoptive relationships. That is, adoptive parents should discuss openly with their adopted children the fact that both parties have reasons to be sad: the children have lost their biological parents, and the adoptive parents (usually) have been denied the opportunity to have a biological child. Kirk asserts that this "acknowledgment-of-difference" approach allows children to relax, compared to the typical "rejection-of-difference" approach, which creates anxiety and ambiguity for both parties. Furthermore, the acknowledgment of loss is a shared experience, which may strengthen the relationship between children and their adoptive parents [Kirk 1984].

For children in foster care, acknowledgment of the past and open discussion of their loss may come as a relief. It gives them the moratorium mentioned earlier: they do not have to pretend they were born into the foster family in order to be accepted. Foster carers can also acknowledge that there are limits on their commitment, that is, they are sharing parenting responsibilities with an agency and the child's parents, for as long as this is feasible for everyone concerned. The open recognition of uncertainty in the situation allows both parties to be honest, and may thereby increase the chance for a productive placement.

Including Parents in Foster Care

Inclusive foster care is a practice in which caregivers willingly include children's families and workers in the children's lives [Holman 1974]. The foster carers recognize that children's identity depends on knowing their roots, and encourage the children's quest for background information. They often engage in supportive work with the parents, which may continue even after the child has returned home [Steinhauer 1991].

Inclusive foster care was studied empirically in the 1970s: in two studies of foster care by different researchers [Holman 1974; Adamson 1973], 31% of several hundred and 54% of 92 carers, respectively, believed that biological parents should see their children. Since then, almost no empirical research has been published on inclusive/exclusive attitudes. It may be expected, however, that agencies are now encouraging a more inclusive approach, as the importance of parents is a central concept in the permanency planning movement.

The success of inclusiveness depends upon the openness of the foster carers: because the children are in their homes, foster carers generally control access to them by workers and parents. Despite the official power assigned to workers, it may be awkward for them to see children alone when foster carers are uncomfortable with this. The caregivers also have the ultimate power to accept or reject a child. The great influence of foster carers on children's family ties is illustrated by the experience of a family that fostered four emotionally disturbed boys of latency age. At an agency picnic, one of the boys encountered five different sets of previous caregivers, all of whom he called Mom and Dad. The current foster carers were concerned about the unreality of this, and decided they would encourage the boys to use the carers' first names. Within a few weeks, all four boys had taken some initiative to communicate with or find out about their biological families. It seemed that an unspoken taboo had been lifted, allowing them to pursue their underlying concerns.

The inclusive approach has the major advantage of encouraging teamwork between caregivers and parents, increasing the chance of placement success. "The stability of planned long-term foster care is partly contingent upon parental agreement that this is the best arrangement for their children" [Gambrill & Stein 1985: 175]. "Clinical experience indicates that resistant children adjust more quickly when parents they love are able to give them permission to accept the foster home" [Fine 1985: 213]. Experience with group care has shown that "residential facilities can be much more effective when they are perceived as a component of the solution to family dysfunction, not as a substitute for families who have failed" [Gibson & Noble 1991: 371].

A pattern of cooperation between the child's two homes can be established from the outset by including parents in preplacement visits [Finkelstein 1980]. Some residential programs have used contracts involving children, parents, and caregivers to establish routines of parental visiting and communication [Van Hagen 1983] and to give parents a clearly stated role in their children's care [Blumenthal 1984]. In an early approach to contracting with foster carers, social workers included parents and children over age six with foster carers in formulating an agreement about the conditions that would govern the placement [Galaway 1976]. The contract included the reason why the placement was necessary, the goals of the placement, plans to maintain family involvement, and plans for regular communication among foster carers, parents, and social worker. This approach has important strengths: it increases the chances of obtaining cooperation from parents and children who have helped in the contracting, improves children's understanding of the reasons for placement, which has been shown to improve their adjustment in care [Thorpe 1974], and reinforces parental responsibility by spelling out tasks to keep parents involved with their children, such as buying clothing, helping to establish rules, and meeting with caregivers regarding the handling of children's behavior problems [Jenson & Whittaker 1987]. Assigning a child care role to the parents has been found to hasten a child's exit from care [Stein et al. 1978].

As mentioned above, some programs are being developed in which foster carers provide parental skills training to biological parents. Preliminary results with one such program indicated that parents responded positively to being involved with foster carers in this way, and that most parents had their children returned to them within eight weeks [Kellerman 1992].

The inclusive model of fostering has clearly achieved recognition in terms of theory and practice principles. Yet exclusive attitudes and practices persist, as shown above. Commitment to change must be followed by concrete action on the part of agencies. One key to change is to treat all foster carers as paraprofessionals, encouraging them to approach children's families more as enablers than as competitors. The other keys to change are the attitudes of workers and the agency context in which they function; the relevant research is reviewed below.

Workers: The Complexity and Potential of Their Role

Difficulty and Complexity of Child Protection

The work of child protection practitioners can be very taxing. Workers tend to have heavy caseloads; their role in separating children from their families is likely to be emotionally draining; competing demands draw them away from families after children are placed; and they have to balance their roles of helping children and representing authority.

Heavy Workloads. Child protection is widely acknowledged to be one of the most demanding fields of social work. The quantity of the work is onerous: workers are overextended because of inadequate resources and excessive caseloads [Steinhauer 1984]. The nature of child protection presents another type of burden for workers. The families with whom they work tend to have multiple problems and insufficient resources, both material and interpersonal. Moreover, "unrelenting emotional demands [are] placed on the worker by the life and death issues of separation, loss, abuse and neglect" [Germain 1979: 174].

Emotional Drain of Involvement in Separation. The process of separating children from their families can leave workers emotionally burdened by the loss and grief felt by parents and children [Jenkins & Norman 1972]. Although there seem to be no published empirical studies of workers' feelings, the gap between accepted theory and practice suggests that workers approach the separation process with discomfort and uncertainty.

It is clear from theory and research that a great deal of care and preparation is required when children are being separated from their families. Empirical studies of admission practices are lacking, but one study showed that workers dealt with most placements as emergencies, rather than taking the time to find an appropriate home and give children a preplacement visit: 65% of all placements occurred within 48 hours of the request [Steinhauer 1984]. Such haste might be warranted for children being rescued from abusive parents, but most admissions are carried out with parental acceptance: a study in two Ontario CASs showed that 50% of 151 recent admissions were requested, and an additional 23% were "accepted" by parents [Palmer 1983a].

The reasons given by workers for moving children without preplacement visits refer to the feelings of adults and to the workers' time constraints. In the author's experience as a supervisor, workers tended to react in almost a knee-jerk fashion to the demands of community people, parents, foster carers, or their own anxiety to move a child out of a poor situation. When questioned, their attitude seemed to be that children should not be left for even one more day in a home that has been designated as unsuitable for them. For example, Billy's worker turned his preplacement visit to an adoptive home into an emergency placement because the foster father in the home he was leaving was expressing pain to Billy about losing him [Kirk 1984].

When workers respond to such pressures, they are giving priority to their own needs or those of the person requesting the move: most children would be better left in a familiar, if inadequate, situation while being properly prepared for a move [Steinhauer 1984]. As for time constraints, several workers independently told the author, during research conducted in Canada and Britain [Palmer 1992], that they had no time to conduct placement according to recommended principles. They seemed to feel that the limits on their time and resources forced them to work in a response-to-crisis mode.

Emergency-style placements may be part of a survival pattern developed by workers to deal with the emotional pressures of carrying out a separation. One way for workers to deal with the chaos in their environment is to react quickly to parents' request for placement [O'Hagan 1986]. A quick response to someone else's request allows the worker to shortcut the agonizing process of making and carrying out a difficult decision. Gradual moves, with parental accompaniment, place increased strain on workers, but they give children the time and opportunity to express their pain.

All these explanations for treating placements as emergencies emphasize the needs of others over those of the child. It seems that children's best interests tend to be forgotten in the stressful process of separating them from their families.

Competing Demands on Workers after Children are Placed. Workers usually plan to work closely with children's families after placement, both to facilitate communication and to work toward reuniting the families. These plans are often aborted, however, by other claims on the worker's time and by complications arising from family contact.

In a typical case, the foster care worker's efforts center on the children's relationship with the new family...The visiting of the natural parent(s) often becomes the most potentially flammable issue, the one requiring the most sensitive work. Mrs. J. (the mother) begins to fade as a central part of the case, her visits taper off, she seems disinterested. [Laird 1979: 178-9]

Studies over the years have confirmed the tendency toward diminished contact between workers and families after placement [Holman 1973; Gruber 1978; Gambrill & Stein 1985]. As time passes, there is a high risk that contact will stop completely: in a study of children who had been in care for two years, there was "virtually no communication" by social workers with one-third of the mothers and four-fifths of the fathers [Millham et al. 1986: 184].

From the workers' perspective, there are several reasons for giving low priority to the families of placed children. First, the placement process demands a tremendous outlay of concentrated effort, forcing workers to ignore their other cases. By the time the child has been placed, other crises will have developed and begun to claim the workers' attention. Second, the foster home becomes the locale for ongoing work with the child, so casework tends to be centered there rather than with the biological family [Steinhauer 1984]. Third, the children's families may be difficult to track: multiproblem families tend to experience frequent changes in family status—separations, reconstitutions, moves—that make it difficult for workers to stay involved [Millham et al. 1986].

In planning to work with families during placement, workers should acknowledge that there will be competing demands for their time. Unless they set up a plan for ongoing contact at the outset and have a strong commitment to carrying it out, their work with families may easily be allowed to lapse.

Complexity of Combining Authority with Helping. Workers in child protection are expected to combine authority and supportiveness in their work with parents, which creates complex and conflicting demands on them [Hilgendorf 1981]. When parents resist placement, workers will probably have to take part in an adversarial court hearing. If the worker is granted a period of several months custody of the child, she is expected to develop a good working relationship with the parents to help them improve conditions, with the goal of returning their child.

To build relationships under such complex conditions, workers would ideally discuss their authority and elicit the parents' feelings about the power of the agency over their lives. Social workers are typically people who do not seek authority, however, and they tend to minimize this aspect of their role [Palmer 1983b]. Child welfare workers, moreover, may feel somewhat powerless because of their everyday work experiences: they tend to be overloaded, they usually work in bureaucracies that limit their autonomy, and many of their clients are overwhelmed by environmental circumstances that are difficult to change.

Workers do have considerable power in case decisions [Packman et al. 1986; Millham et al. 1986], but they may view this as a burden rather than a strength of their role. A survey of lawyers and court records revealed that many social workers expressed anxiety and uncertainty about the decision to take a child into care, but did not realize the true complexity of their position, and were not given adequate support [Hilgendorf 1981]. In effect, child welfare workers have more power than they may acknowledge, and must deal with this in their work with families, as it can be a major impediment to a good working relationship.

Worker Ambivalence toward Family Involvement with Placed Children

Persistent Conditions That Discourage Involvement. Early studies noted the tendency of social workers to discourage parental visiting, viewing it as a threat to the child's relationship with the foster carers [George 1970; Thorpe 1974; Holman 1974; Gruber 1978]. Now that research has shown the importance of family contact to permanency planning [Fanshel & Shinn 1978], and parental rights are supported by legislation, many agencies have modified their official policies [Stein & Gambrill 1985]. Yet there is continuing evidence of exclusive practice, including the use of distant or inaccessible placements, the process of moving the child, the arrangements for visiting, the exclusion of parents from planning, and general inattention to parents.

In terms of distance of placements from children's biological families, CASs in Ontario's smaller cities draw many of their foster homes from the surrounding countryside, where there is no public transportation to enable parents to visit. In a British study of 450 families, distance was an impediment to visiting for 33% of families [Millham et al. 1986]. As for the process of moving children to a new home, "whenever possible, parents should help the foster parents and share with the foster parents the child's current needs, developmental history, and other relevant information" [CWLA 1995: 27]; children should be accompanied by their parents to the new placement [NFCA 1987]. Yet the few available statistics indicate that this is far from common practice, although it may be increasing. Among 167 children admitted to the care of two Ontario CASs between 1980 and 1981, only 11% had been accompanied by parents when they left home [Palmer 1983a]. A later Ontario CAS study found a rate of 14% parent accompaniment for 73 children in care during 1987 and 1988 who had been in care an average of four years [Kufeldt et al. 1989].

Restrictions are often placed on parental visiting. One reason commonly given is that children should have a period of no visiting so that they can "adjust" to the foster home [Proch & Hess 1987]. Rowe et al. [1984: 99] comment:

We were frequently dismayed and sometimes angered by the ways in which social workers so often failed to provide the necessary support and encouragement to maintain visiting. Sometimes they actually seemed to set up "no win" situations for natural parents, first discouraging visits "to let the child settle" and later saying that, after such a long gap, renewed visiting would be upsetting.

Ongoing family contact is further discouraged by restrictive visiting arrangements, in which families are prevented from going to the foster home or having their children come home overnight; instead, they are limited to office visiting during normal working hours [Borgman 1985]. Furthermore, restrictions on family contact in specific cases have been found to increase over time [Millham et al. 1986]. In arranging visits, workers and agencies tend to give precedence to the routines of foster carers, rather than those of the family [Berridge & Cleaver 1987; Jenson & Whittaker 1987].

Parents tend to be left out of planning for their children in care. They often do not understand the legal implications of agency custody; are excluded, for the most part, from planning meetings; and receive little written confirmation of decisions [Tunnard 1989]. Furthermore, they are often unclear about the implications if they accept, or fail to challenge, agency actions [Tunnard 1989]. Parents are not usually included in, or even kept informed about, decisions regarding their children [Millham et al. 1986]; in particular, they are excluded from most decisions about moves or choice of foster home [Kufeldt et al. 1989].

Finally, workers tend to minimize the importance of parents in their general approach to foster care. As noted above, contact with families after placement is often allowed to lapse, and little support is given to parental visiting [Hess 1988]. The typical attitude to the families of placed children has been described as "studied indifference" [Schatz & Bane 1991: 676]. An example of children's families being ignored was found by the author in the course of researching case records: a few files contained letters from parents addressed to their children, expressing their concern and affection. These letters had been opened, but apparently not delivered. There was no explanation for this in the case record.

Possible Motives for Excluding Families. The literature suggests many possible reasons why workers may exclude families from their children's placement experience: a desire to give children a "fresh start," protectiveness toward the placement, noncooperation from parents, burnout in relation to a particular family, and lack of time and energy.

Traditionally, agencies discouraged parental visiting in the belief that the lack of visits would allow neglected and abused children to make a fresh start in foster care. Their belief was reinforced by the passive response of most parents to being excluded [George 1970: 181]. As described by George, social workers and foster carers

> by their active hostility or passive inaction toward natural parents have forced or have merely allowed natural parents to alienate themselves from their children. This alienation has in turn been used as evidence for the natural parents' lack of interest in their children and for their inability to care for them adequately. [1970: 220]

Vestiges of this traditional view remain with us. Researchers have commented on "the anti-family ideology that is the historical legacy of social work and still pervades the service" [Berridge & Cleaver 1987: 76]. Workers may exclude parents in the hope that children "will be spared from being repeatedly upset and will eventually forget them, freeing [them] to form a secure attachment to the foster parents" [Steinhauer 1991: 163].

Workers may collude with foster carers, who hold a bias in favor of exclusiveness, for fear of endangering the placement [Holman 1974]. Researchers have found that some workers overestimate the disruptive potential of parental visits [Millham et al. 1986]. Workers may confuse disruption to foster carers with damage to children: in a survey of foster carers, many said that allowing children to go home for visits was disruptive and distressing for themselves and the children, implying that home visits should be reduced [Simms & Bolden 1991]. The children may have shown distress, but this does not necessarily mean they would prefer not to go home for visits. It is more likely that disturbed behavior by children reflects a conflict of loyalties between their parents and their foster carers [Gean et al. 1985]. If foster carers were more willing to have visits, the children might be less distressed. As confirmed by a study of families separated by divorce, continued contact with a noncustodial parent can be beneficial when the custodial parent is willing to cooperate in the interests of the child [Wallerstein & Blakeslee 1989].

Parents are often unreliable about keeping appointments. An informal survey by the author, during training sessions with placement workers, indicated that about 25% of planned visits are missed by the parents. This accords with the findings of an assisted visiting program: cancellations and no-shows averaged 25% over two years [Hess et al. 1992]. The primary problems were transportation and ambivalence about visiting, on the part of both parents and foster carers, as well as the latter's "scheduling" problems, and children's illnesses.

Workers may become discouraged with parents who are inconsistent in their visiting; wishing to protect a child from disappointment, the worker may allow contact to lapse. This may not be the best solution: in view of children's tendency to idealize absent parents, they may view their parents' apparent lack of interest as reflecting their own unworthiness. Sporadic contact may be better than none at all: the experience of cancellations and no-shows may be painful for children, but it can help them to maintain a realistic picture of their parents' inherent limitations [Steinhauer 1991]. Additional structure and support may be needed for families with poor visiting patterns. A structured visiting program reported increased frequency and consistency of contact between parents and children when agencies took the initiative and built in supports [Hess et al. 1992].

Over time, workers may begin to feel burned out in their relationship with some families. When workers struggle to help a family stay together, they may have a sense of failure when they are eventually forced to give up and bring the children into care.

This may cause them to undervalue the family's potential to offer support to the child during placement.

> The failure of preventive work with families and the consequent separation of children on entry to care are viewed as signal defeats by social workers ... Consequently, the family is seldom viewed as a resource. [Millham et al. 1986: 106]

Psychologically, workers find it stressful to maintain the link between children and their parents [Millham et al. 1986]. In the author's experience with child placement, inner conflict is generated by the process of trying to rejoin two parts of a whole that one has been instrumental in splitting. Workers may also experience burnout with parents who are alienated and behave in an uncooperative or hostile manner with them. Such behavior may cause workers to lose respect for the parents, and consequently to underestimate their continuing importance to their children in care [Steinhauer 1991].

Finally, workers may discourage visiting through default rather than active intervention [Rowe et al. 1984]. They may limit access because they believe this is the agency norm: a study of visiting practices found that some workers who asked parents not to visit could not identify what harm they expected from visiting [Gibson & Parsloe 1984]. Or they may be dealing with a demanding caseload, and take the path of least resistance; they are less likely to be "hassled" by a family who is being ignored than by a foster carer or child who is not receiving sufficient attention. Bureaucratic expectations also pull workers toward foster carers and children, rather than toward the children's parents: legislation and standards usually set minimum levels for workers' contact with children, but the level of family contact is left to workers' discretion. Overall, workers and caregivers alike place insufficient value on parental ties and make too little effort to maintain them [Stein et al. 1978].

In the process of protecting children, parents' strengths and commitment to their children may be undervalued, and their involvement discouraged. Parents can continue to take a meaningful role in their children's lives after placement, if workers take care not to push them aside or devalue their importance.

Fear of Attempting Reunion. Agencies and workers seem to feel they have failed if a planned reunion of children with their families ends in reentry to care: even the literature uses the negative-sounding term *recidivism*. From the child's viewpoint, however, an attempted reunion may sometimes be the best choice. Empirical findings suggest that foster placements are more likely than reunions to break down. A comparative study of 187 children found that 50% of moves to long-term foster homes were disrupted, compared to 32% of moves back to biological families [Fein et al. 1983]. Interestingly, the latter rate was the same as that for adoptive placements [Fein et al. 1979]. Another finding supporting trial reunions is that children who had gone home and then returned to care functioned better than those who had never been returned home [Fein et al. 1983].

These findings support the assertion that "the effects on children of a temporary return to their biological parents, with the overall aim of pursuing permanency planning, does not lead to the dire effects on children supposed" [Gambrill & Stein 1985: 175]. Moreover, support services to families can contribute greatly to the success of a reunion. A comparison of children who reentered care after being returned to their families with children who did not reenter care showed that the latter group received casework services for a significantly longer time [Turner 1984].

Selective Inattention to Children's Past Experiences

Despite theoretical recognition of children's early family experiences as basic to their ongoing relationships, workers tend to center their interest on the here-and-now. In one study, only 18% of 119 workers felt they had primary responsibility for sharing family history with children [Rowe et al. 1984]; they apparently expected foster carers to do this, yet the latter were found to have a "striking" lack of information. Moreover, foster carers also shrink from talking to children about the past: in a program featuring structured agency discussion with foster carers, they were assessed as being "aware of the psychological burden experienced by the children for whom they were caring. They felt overwhelmed and overburdened...and deeply concerned about opening a Pandora's box" [Rice & McFadden 1988: 240].

The implication of workers' inattention to a child's past attachments and trauma is that these will be forgotten if only the right placement can be found.

> The child welfare system has been...ignoring the potency of children's prior experiences with families, believing that a certain type of environment in the here and now will "treat" a child if fundamental family connections are left unaddressed, and pretending that in moving a child from one setting to another we are solving problems. [McFadden 1993]

A consultant psychiatrist noted that workers and foster carers alike tended to treat children's underlying separation feelings with selective inattention, if not active discouragement [Steinhauer 1974]. Children are expected to be happy or grateful for their placements and are discouraged from expressing sadness [Campbell 1991].

Workers should stop ignoring children's feelings and offer them the help they need. Many children in care are experiencing "unwanted and unbearable feelings" and can be helped by a worker who will "put [their feelings] into words... turning them into something that can be tolerated and finally incorporated into a child's identity" [Simmonds 1988: 19].

Potential to Empower Families and Children

Competence and Opportunity. Considering the complexities of out-of-home placement, and the divergent interests of the parties, the worker's role is crucial. Ideally, the worker will have the knowledge and skill to understand and draw out the feelings of parents and children, support their relationship during separation, and facilitate the foster carers' acceptance of this [Wald et al. 1988]. These tasks are suited to the competence of professional social workers: "Unlike so many variables in the family and care situation of [the] children, all of which defy social work interventions, keeping links going is well within social workers' capabilities" [Millham et al. 1986: 116].

In terms of opportunity, workers are in a pivotal position to carry out the above tasks. Ideally, the same worker will continue working with parents and children throughout the placement experience; this gives a worker many opportunities to respond to children's separation feelings and to enlist parents in explaining events to them. Children's feelings are likely to be most accessible during the preparation for placement and the separation itself, when the worker is constantly with them. Further opportunities will be presented during the placement, because the child's mourning over separation takes place sporadically, over time [Steinhauer 1984: 477].

An important part of the worker's role derives from her power to influence the child-parent relationship during a placement. Although parental access is usually supported by a court order, the worker becomes the court-delegated agent, as it were, who initiates planning and interprets agency norms for biological and foster families. The planning function includes the development, implementation, and monitoring of visiting arrangements [Hess 1987]. The centrality of the worker is confirmed by research findings: parents tend to visit as often as allowed by the plan developed under the worker's leadership [Proch & Howard 1986]; the frequency of parent-child visiting varies with the worker's investment in the case [Fanshel & Shinn 1978]. Finally, the parents often need the worker's help to overcome obstacles to visiting that are created by the turbulence and change in their own lives [Millham et al. 1986].

Methods of Empowerment. Workers can share power

with children and their families by giving them as much information as possible and ensuring their participation in decision making. This facilitates their active involvement in working toward reunion; it also increases their self-esteem by giving them a sense of control over their own lives [Schatz & Bane 1991].

The evidence presented earlier indicates that although many children have large gaps in self-knowledge about the past, their families, and why they are in care, workers and caregivers appear reluctant to discuss these subjects with children. Children's own parents are likely to be their most credible source of information, and workers should help parents to talk with their children about the events leading to their placement [Adcock 1983]. This can be done verbally, in a playroom setting (with the worker's guidance), or by having parents work on a life story book with their children. If the worker assumes this task unilaterally, parents are likely to feel excluded and powerless [Adcock 1983].

Children can also be empowered by being given information about their legal rights. In some jurisdictions, these rights include the right to appeal the placement selected for them, to choose their own religion, and to communicate privately with their families [Ontario 1984]. Involvement of children and youths in making decisions about their lives helps to ensure their commitment to carry out those decisions. One program involved young people in their own case planning, as well as focusing on their positive qualities, and placing them with, or near, relatives whenever possible: the result was a decrease in placement breakdown [Taber & Proch 1987].

Children may also gain power by participating in support groups with others in similar circumstances. In treatment groups focused on separation, children discussed feelings they had never revealed to their workers or caregivers [Palmer 1990]. The resolution of separation feelings through group therapy has been shown with children who have lost parents through divorce or death. They "appear less constricted and angry over time, and seem much more able to understand and cope with the emotional reactions they have had and are continuing to experience" [Masterman & Reams 1988: 569].

Several principles for empowering parents were identified by a program committed to maintaining families' involvement with their children in care [Schatz & Bane 1991]. Parents were encouraged to continue carrying parental responsibilities, to value themselves as caregivers, and to advocate for their children's needs. This accords with the principles of inclusive foster care, in which parents and caregivers cooperate to care for a child.

> The involvement of biological parents in children's residential care is the most critical component in the evolution of family-based group care services. Residential settings must be viewed as a support system for those families who wish to maintain their child in the home, not as substitute placements for families who have failed. [Jenson & Whittaker 1987]

Keeping parents informed about their children in care is a basic form of empowerment. Research suggests that information-sharing with parents is deficient: of 170 children, the whereabouts of 23% were unknown to their mothers after two years in care; this figure increased to 37% for fathers [Millham et al. 1986]. In some cases, agencies may be trying to protect children from abusive parents, but this does not account for the degree or duration of exclusion indicated by these statistics. From the viewpoint of children as well, it must be a lonely experience to realize that their families do not know their whereabouts.

Parental rights have been increasingly recognized by legislation, including provisions for legal counsel, participation in decision-making, and access to children [Stein & Gambrill 1985]. Despite these legislative advances, researchers have found that neither parents nor children were involved very much in determining the frequency or location of visits [Proch & Hess 1987].

Workers undoubtedly find it cumbersome to include parents and children in decision-making, especially when they are not physically present in the agency, but it is a necessary part of supporting parental responsibility and giving children some control over their lives. In the short term, parents' insistence on their rights may pose problems for workers, who find it simpler to work with parents who are compliant. Yet parents who know and insist on their rights may be demonstrating strengths that should be encouraged. If they have enough spirit and energy to resist agency control over their children, this same energy can be used to make changes toward getting their children back.

Parent self-help programs build on the strengths of families, offering parents respect and assistance in accessing the necessary resources to reunite their families [Tunnard 1989]. Offering parents an opportunity to meet in groups is a message from the agency that they are seen as a valuable resource for their children [Levin 1992]. It may be difficult to involve families who have been alienated by their experiences in society. Agencies that have persisted in offering group experiences, however, report that parents benefit from the opportunity of sharing painful experiences, asserting their anger, supporting each other's progress, and learning from each other's reports of success [Levin 1992].

Discussion

As this literature review shows, many aspects of placement practice fall short of meeting children's needs for attachment, identity, and continuity. Despite the critical lack of resources in child welfare, however, there are possibilities for change in the attitudes of workers and foster carers. In particular, workers and foster carers should give increased priority to family ties and to the need of children to understand their pasts.

The literature provides strong support for an inclusive approach to foster care, in terms of both accepted principles and empirical research. Despite the long-established depth, consistency, and unanimity of these principles and of the knowledge base in general, families are still being excluded from their children's lives, and children lack basic information about their families. Children and their families must be given additional control over the placement experience. With empowerment, children will be increasingly likely to express their needs and parents will be encouraged to continue being responsible for their children. A solid beginning has been made in developing programs that support inclusive fostering; it is time to put to work what we have known for a long time.

References

Adamson, G. (1973). *The caretakers*. London: Bookstall Publications.

Adcock, M. (1983). Working with natural parents to prevent long-term care. *Adoption and Fostering, 7*(5), 8–12.

Allen, M., Bonner, K., & Greenan, L. (1988). Federal legislative support for independent living. *Child Welfare, 67*, 515–527.

Anderson, J. L., & Simonitch, B. (1981). Reactive depression in youths experiencing emancipation. *Child Welfare, 60*, 383–390.

Astrachan, M., & Harris, D.M. (1983). Weekend only: An alternate model in residential treatment centers. *Child Welfare, 62*, 253–261.

Balbernie, R. (1974). Unintegration, integration and level of ego functioning as the determinants of planned "cover therapy," of unit task, and of placement. *Association of Workers for Maladjusted Children Journal, 2*, 6–46.

Barr, D.H. (1971, October). "Doing prevention" in Regent Park. *Journal of the Ontario Association of Children's Aid Societies, 14*, 8–13.

Barth, R.P., & Berry, M. (1990). A decade later: Outcomes of permanency planning. In North American Council on Adoptable Children (Ed.), *The Adoption Assistance and Child Welfare Act of 1980: The first ten years*. St Paul, MN: North American Council on Adoptable Children.

Berridge, D., & Cleaver, H. (1987). *Foster home breakdown*. Oxford, England: Basil Blackwell

Beste, H.M., & Richardson, R.G. (1981). Developing a life story book program for foster children. *Child Welfare, 60*, 529–534.

Block, N.M. (1981). Toward reducing recidivism in foster care. *Child Welfare, 60*, 597–609.

Blumenthal, K. (1984). Involving parents: A rationale. In K. Blumenthal & A. Weinberg (Eds.), *Establishing parental involvement in foster care agencies* (pp. 1–16). New York: Child Welfare League of America.

Borgman, R. (1985). The influence of family visiting upon boys' behavior in a juvenile correctional institution. *Child Welfare, 64*, 629–638.

Boszormenyi-Nagy, I. (1973). *Invisible loyalties: Reciprocity in intergenerational family therapy*. Hagerstown, MD: Harper and Row.

Boyd, P.E. (1979). They can go home again. *Child Welfare, 58*, 609–615.

Campbell, K. (1991). The use of videotape in the separation and grief process for children in long-term foster care and adoption. Toronto, ON: Institute for the Prevention of Child Abuse.

Cantrell, D. (1988). Front-line turnover. *Journal of the Ontario Association of Children's Aid Societies, 32*, 2–9.

Cautley, P.W. (1980) *New foster parents: The first experience*. New York: Human Sciences Press.

Chamberlain, P., Moreland, S., & Reid, K. (1992). Enhanced services and stipends for foster parents: Effects on retention rates and outcomes for children. *Child Welfare, 71*, 387–401.

Child Welfare League of America. (1995). *Standards of excellence for family foster care services*. Washington, DC: Author.

Cimmarusti, R.A. (1992). Family preservation practice based upon a multisystems approach. *Child Welfare, 71*, 241–256.

Close, M.M. (1983). Child welfare and people of color: Denial of equal access. *Social Work Research and Abstracts, 19*, 13–20.

Crown Ward Administrative Review. (1991). *Report for 1989 and 1990*. Toronto, ON: Crown Ward Review Unit, Ontario Ministry of Community and Social Services.

Dubowitz, H., Feigelman, S., & Zuravin, S. (1993). A profile of kinship care. *Child Welfare, 72*, 153–169.

Eisenberg, L. (1962). The sins of the fathers: Urban decay and social pathology. *American Journal of Orthopsychiatry, 32*, 5–17.

Fahlberg, V. (1985). *Attachment and separation*. London: British Agencies for Adoption and Fostering.

Fanshel, D., & Shinn, E.B. (1978). *Children in foster care: A longitudinal investigation*. New York: Columbia University Press.

Fanshel, D. (1981). Foreword. In A. Maluccio & P.A. Sinanoglu (Eds.), *The challenge of partnership*. New York: Child Welfare League of America.

Fanshel, D. (1982). *On the road to permanency: An expanded data base for service to children in foster care*. New York: Child Welfare League of America.

Fanshel, D., Finch, S.J., & Grundy, J.F. (1989). Foster children in life-course perspective: The Casey Family Program experience. *Child Welfare, 68*, 467–478.

Fein, E., Davies, L., & Knight, G. (1979). Placement stability in foster care. *Social Work, 24*, 156–157.

Fein, E., Maluccio, A.N., Hamilton, V.J., & Ward, D.E. (1983). After foster care: Outcomes of permanency planning for children. *Child Welfare, 62*, 485–558.

Fein, E., & Staff, I. (1991). Implementing reunification services. *Families in Society, 72*, 335–343.

Fein, E., & Maluccio, A.N. (1992). Permanency planning: Another remedy in jeopardy? *Social Service Review, 66*, 335–348.

Festinger, T. (1983). *No one ever asked us.... A postscript to foster care*. New York: Columbia University Press.

Fine, P. (1985). Clinical aspects of foster care. In M.J. Cox & R.D. Cox (Eds.), *Foster care: Current issues, policies, and practices* (pp. 206–233). Norwood, NY: Ablex Publishing.

Finkelstein, N.E. (1980). Family-centered group care. *Child Welfare, 59*, 33–41.

Fisher, M., Marsh, P., Phillips, D., & Sainsbury, E. (1986). *In and out of care: The experience of children, parents and social workers*. Batsford, England: British Agencies for Adoption & Fostering.

Fitzgerald, J. (1982). *Building new families through adoption and fostering*. Oxford, England: Basil Blackwell.

Gabinet, L. (1983). Shared parenting: A new paradigm for the treatment of child abuse. *Child Abuse and Neglect, 7*, 403–411.

Galaway, B. Contracting: A means of clarifying roles in foster family services. *Children Today, 5*, 20–23.

Gambrill, E., & Stein, T. (1985). Working with biological parents: Important procedural ingredients. *Children and Youth Services Review, 7*, 173–189.

Gean, M.P., Gillmore, J.L., & Dowler, J.K. (1985). Infants and toddlers in supervised custody: A pilot study of visitation. *Journal of the American Academy of Child Psychiatry, 24*, 609–612.

Geiser, C. (1973). *The illusion of caring: Children in foster care.* Boston: Beacon Press.

George, V. (1970). *Foster care: Theory and practice.* London: Routledge and Kegan Paul.

Germain, C. (1979). Editor's introduction to J. Laird, An ecological approach to child welfare: Issues of family identity and continuity. In C. Germain, (Ed.), *People and environments* (pp. 174–209). New York: Columbia University Press.

Gibson, D., & Noble, D.N. (1991). Creative permanency planning: Residential services for families. *Child Welfare, 70*, 371–382.

Gibson, P., & Parsloe, P. (1984). What stops parental access to children in care? *Adoption and Fostering, 8*, 18–24.

Gruber, A.R. (1978). *Children in foster care: Destitute, neglected, betrayed.* New York: Human Sciences Press.

Hamilton-Wentworth. (1990). *Parent-adolescent support service.* Pamphlet available from Hamilton-Wentworth Children's Aid Society.

Hardin, M. (1988). New legal options to prepare adolescents for community living. *Child Welfare, 67*, 529–546.

Hess, P. (1987). Parental visiting of children in foster care. *Children and Youth Services Review, 9*, 29–50.

Hess, P. (1988). Case and context: Determinants of planned visit frequency in foster family care. *Child Welfare, 67*, 311–326.

Hess, P., Mintun, G., Moelhman, A., & Pitts, G. (1992). The family connection center: An innovative visiting program. *Child Welfare, 71*, 77–88.

Hilgendorf, L. (1981). *Social workers and solicitors in child care cases.* London: Her Majesty's Stationery Office.

Hinton, S. (1978). On being a foster child. *Journal of the Ontario Association of Children's Aid Societies, 21*, 9–10.

Holman, R. (1973). *Trading in children*. London: Routledge and Kegan Paul.

Holman, R. (1975). The place of fostering in social work. *British Journal of Social Work, 5*, 3–29.

Irvine, J. (1988). Aftercare services. *Child Welfare, 67*, 587–594.

Jenkins, S., & Norman, E. (1972). *Filial deprivation and foster care*. New York: Columbia University Press.

Jenkins, S., & Norman, E. (1975). *Beyond placement: Mothers view foster care*. New York: Columbia University Press.

Jenkins, R. (1969). Long term fostering. *Case Conference, 15*, 349–353.

Jenson, J.M., & Whittaker, J.K. (1987). Parental involvement in children's residential treatment: From preplacement to after care. *Children and Youth Services Review, 9*, 81–100.

Jones, M.A. (1985). *A second chance for families: Five years later. Follow-up of a program to prevent foster care*. New York: Child Welfare League of America.

Jones, M.A., & Moses, B. (1984). *West Virginia's former foster children: Their experience in care and their lives as young adults*. New York: Child Welfare League of America.

Kahan, B. (1979). *Growing up in care: Ten people talking*. Oxford, England: Basil Blackwell.

Kellerman, S.S. (1992). Foster parents as teachers and parent aides. *Journal of the Ontario Association of Children's Aid Societies, 36*, 14–17.

Kemp, C.J. (1971). Family treatment within the milieu of residential treatment centers. *Child Welfare, 50*, 229–235.

Kinney, J., Haapala, D., Booth, C., & Leavitt, S. (1990). The Homebuilders model. In J. Whittaker, J. Kinney, E. Tracy, & C. Booth (Eds.), *Reaching high-risk families: Intensive family preservation in human services* (pp. 31–64). New York: Aldine de Gruyter.

Kirk, H.D. (1984). *Shared fate: A theory and method of adoptive relationships* (rev. ed.). Brentwood Bay, BC: Ben-Simon Publications.

Kufeldt, K., Armstrong, J., & Dorosh, M. (1989). In care, in contact? In

J. Hudson & B. Galaway (Eds.), *The state as parent* (pp. 355–368). Dordrecht, Netherlands: Kluwer Academic Publishers.

Lahti, J., Green, K., Emlen, A., Zendry, J., Clarkson, Q.D., Kuehnel, M., & Casciato, J. (1978). *A follow-up study of the Oregon project.* Portland, OR: Regional Research for Human Services, Portland State University.

Lawder, E.A., Poulin, J.E., & Andrews, R.G. (1986). A study of 185 children 5 years after placement. *Child Welfare, 65,* 241–251.

Lee, J.A.B., & Nisivoccia, D. (1989). *Walk a mile in my shoes.* Washington, DC: Child Welfare League of America.

Levin, A.E. (1992). Groupwork with parents in the family foster care system: A powerful method of engagement. *Child Welfare, 71,* 457–473.

Levin, S., Rubenstein, J.S., & Streiner, D.L. (1976). The parent therapist program: An innovative approach to treating emotionally disturbed children. *Hospital and Community Psychiatry, 27,* 407–410.

Levitt, K. (1981). A Canadian approach to permanent planning. *Child Welfare, 60,* 109–112.

Lewis, R.E., & Fraser, M. (1987). Blending informal and formal helping networks in foster care. *Children and Youth Services Review, 9,* 153–169.

Lindsey, D. (1991). Factors affecting the foster care placement decision: An analysis of national survey data. *American Journal of Orthopsychiatry, 61,* 272–81.

Loewe, B., & Hanrahan, T.E. (1975). Day foster care. *Child Welfare, 54,* 7–18.

Lowe, M.I. (1991). The challenge of partnership: A national foster care charter in the United Kingdom. *Child Welfare, 70,* 151–156.

MacDonald, G.D. (1992). Accepting parental responsibility: "Future questioning" as a means to avoid foster home placement of children. *Child Welfare, 71,* 3–17.

Main, M., Kaplan, N., & Cassidy, J. (1985). Security in infancy, childhood and adulthood: A move to the level of representation. In I. Bretherton & E. Waters (Eds.), Growing points of attachment theory and research. *Monographs of the Society for Research in Child Development (Serial No. 209), 50,* 66–104.

Maluccio, A.N., & Fein, E. (1983). Permanency planning: A redefinition. *Child Welfare, 62*, 195–201.

Maluccio, A.N., & Sinanoglu, P.A. (Eds.). (1981). *The challenge of partnership*. New York: Child Welfare League of America.

Mannes, M. (1993). Seeking the balance between child protection and family preservation in Indian child welfare. *Child Welfare, 72*, 141–152,

Masterman, S.H., & Reams, R. (1988). Support groups for bereaved preschool and school-age children. *American Journal of Orthopsychiatry, 58*, 562–570.

McAdams, P. (1972). The parent in the shadows. *Child Welfare, 51*, 51–55.

McFadden, E.J. (1993, Summer). Response to the FFTA's discussion paper re permanency. *Foster Family-based Treatment Association Newsletter*, p. 9.

Meadowcroft, P., & Trout, B.A. (1990). *Troubled youth in treatment homes: A handbook of therapeutic foster care*. Washington, DC: Child Welfare League of America.

Mech, E.V. (1985). Parental visiting and foster placement. *Child Welfare, 64*, 67–72.

Meston, J. (1988). Preparing young people in Canada for emancipation from child welfare care. *Child Welfare, 67*, 625–634.

Meyer, C (1984). Editorial: Can foster care be saved? *Social Work, 29*, 499.

Michaels, K.W., & Green, R.H. (1979). A child welfare agency project: Therapy for families of status offenders. *Child Welfare, 58*, 216–220.

Millham, S., Bullock, R., Hosie, K., & Haak, M.. (1986). *Lost in care*. London: Gower.

National Foster Care Association (NFCA). (1987). *Foster care charter*. London: Author.

National Foster Care Association (NFCA). (1988). The challenge of foster care. Transcript of videotape of foster children's experiences.

O'Hagan, K. (1986). *Crisis intervention in social services*. Hong Kong: MacMillan Education.

Ontario Association of Children's Aid Societies. (1971, April). The feelings of a foster child. *Journal of the Ontario Association of Children's Aid Societies, 14*, 15–16.

Ontario Association of Children's Aid Societies. (1988, September). OACAS staff report: We are real people too! *Journal of the Ontario Association of Children's Aid Societies, 32*, 2–11.

Ontario Child and Family Services Act 1984.

Packman, J., Randall, J., & Jacques, N. (1986). *Who needs care? Social work decisions about children.* Oxford, England: Basil Blackwell.

Palmer, S.E. (1976). *Children in long-term care: Their experiences and progress.* London, ON: Family and Children's Services.

Palmer, S.E. (1979). Predicting outcome in long-term foster care. *Journal of Social Service Research, 3*, 201–214.

Palmer, S.E. (1983a). *The effects of training on CAS workers' handling of separation* (doctoral thesis, University of Toronto).

Palmer, S.E. (1983b). Authority: An essential part of social work practice. *Social Work, 28*, 120–125.

Palmer, S.E. (1990). Group treatment with foster children to reduce separation conflicts associated with placement breakdown. *Child Welfare, 69*, 227–238.

Palmer, S.E. (1992). Including birth families in foster care: A Canadian-British comparison. *Children and Youth Services Review, 14*, 407–425.

Pardeck, J.T. (1984). Multiple placement of children in foster family care: An empirical analysis. *Social Work, 29*, 506–509.

Parker, R. (1966). *Decision in child care.* London: Allen and Unwin.

Pavelson, M. (1972, November). Foster daycare: An alternative to admission. *Journal of the Ontario Association of Children's Aid Societies, 15*, 1–4.

Pecora, P.J., Fraser, M.W., & Haapala, D.A. (1992). Intensive home-based family preservation services: An update from the FIT Project. *Child Welfare, 71*, 177–188.

Petrie, J.R.J. (1962). Residential treatment of maladjusted children: A study of some factors related to progress in adjustment. *British Journal of Educational Psychology, 32*, 29–37.

Polansky, N.A., Chalmers, M.A., Williams, D.P., & Buttenwieser, E.W. (1981). *Damaged parents: An anatomy of child neglect.* Chicago: University of Chicago Press.

Proch, K., & Hess, P.M. (1987). Parent-child visiting policies of voluntary agencies. *Children and Youth Services Review, 9,* 17–28.

Proch, K., & Howard, J.A. (1986). Parental visiting of children in foster care: A study of casework practice. *Social Work, 31,* 178–181.

Ralphs, K. (1991, July). Specialist in Foster Care & Adoption, Kent County Local Authority, U.K. Personal communication.

Raychaba, B. (1988). *To be on our own with no direction from home: A report on the special needs of young people leaving the care of the child welfare system.* Ottawa, ON: National Youth in Care Network.

Raychaba, B. (1993). *Pain, lots of pain: Family violence and abuse in the lives of young people in care.* Ottawa, ON: National Youth in Care Network.

Rice, D.L., & McFadden, E.J. (1988). A forum for foster children. *Child Welfare, 67,* 231–243.

Rowe, J., & Lambert, L. (1973). *Children who wait.* London: British Association of Adoption and Fostering.

Rowe, J., Cain, H., Hundleby, M., & Keane, A. (1984). *Long-term foster care.* London: Batsford.

Ryan, P., McFadden, E.J., & Warren, B.L. (1981). Foster families: A resource for helping parents. In A. Maluccio & P. Sinanoglu (Eds.), *The challenge of partnership: Working with parents of children in foster care* (pp. 189–199). New York: Child Welfare League of America.

Ryan, P., McFadden, E.J., Rice, D., & Warren, B. (1988). The role of foster parents in helping young people develop emancipation skills. *Child Welfare, 67,* 563–572.

Savas, S.A., Epstein, I., & Grasso, A.J. (1993). Client characteristics, family contacts, and treatment outcomes. *Child and Youth Services, 16,* 125–137.

Schatz, M.S., & Bane, W. (1991). Empowering the parents of children in substitute care: A training model. *Child Welfare, 70,* 665–678.

Simmonds, J. (1988). Social work with children: Developing a framework for responsible practice. In J. Aldgate & J. Simmonds (Eds.), *Direct work with children* (pp. 1–21). London: Batsford.

Simms, M.D., & Bolden, B.J. (1991). The family reunification project: Facilitating regular contact among foster children, biological families, and foster families. *Child Welfare, 70,* 679–690.

Stein, T.J., & Gambrill, E.D. (1985). Permanency planning for children: The past and present. *Children and Youth Services Review, 7,* 83–94.

Stein, T.J., Gambrill, E.D., & Wiltse, K.T. (1978). *Children in foster homes.* New York: Praeger.

Steinhauer, P. (1974). *How to succeed in the business of creating psychopaths without even trying.* Paper presented to the Annual Meeting of the Ontario Association of Children's Aid Societies, Toronto, ON.

Steinhauer, P. (1984). The management of children admitted to child welfare services in Ontario: A review and discussion of current problems and practices. *Canadian Journal of Psychiatry, 29,* 473–484.

Steinhauer, P. (1991). *The least detrimental alternative: A systematic guide to case planning and decision making for children in care.* Toronto, ON: University of Toronto Press.

Taber, M., & Proch, K. (1987). Placement stability for adolescents in foster care: Findings from a program experiment. *Child Welfare, 66,* 433–445.

"Taking Control" Project. (1985). *Videotape—Searching for My Children.* Regina, SK: University of Saskatchewan.

Thorpe, R. (1974). Mom and Mrs. So and So. *Social Work Today, 4,* 691–695.

Tiddy, S.G. (1986). Creative cooperation: Involving biological parents in long-term foster care. *Child Welfare, 65,* 53–62.

Timms, N. (1973). *The receiving end.* London: Routledge and Kegan Paul.

Titterington, L. (1990). Foster care training: A comprehensive approach. *Child Welfare, 69,* 157–165.

Treen, H. (1964). *A study of permanent wards in the care of Children's Aid Societies in the province of Ontario.* In Report of the Minister's Advisory Committee, Ontario Department of Public Welfare.

Tunnard, J. (1989). Local self-help groups for families of children in public care. *Child Welfare, 68,* 221–227.

Turner, J. (1984). Reuniting children in foster care with their biological parents. *Social Work, 29*, 501–505.

Van Hagen, J. (1983). One residential center's model for working with families. *Child Welfare, 62*, 233–241.

Ville Marie Social Services. (1989, March 30). Case report by social worker during staff training session with author, Montreal, PQ.

Wald, M.S., Carlsmith, J.M., & Leiderman, P.H. (1988). *Protecting abused and neglected children*. Stanford, CA: Stanford University Press.

Wallerstein, J., & Blakeslee, S. (1989). *Second chances: Men, women and children a decade after divorce*. New York: Ticknor and Fields.

Walsh, J.A., & Walsh, R.A. (1990). Studies of the maintenance of subsidized foster placements in the Casey Family Program. *Child Welfare, 69*, 99–114.

Walton, E., Fraser, M.W., Lewis, R.E., Pecora, P.J., & Walter, W.K. (1993). In-home family-focused reunification: An experimental study. *Child Welfare, 72*, 473–487.

Weinstein, E.A. (1960). *The self image of the foster child*. New York: Russell Sage Foundation.

Wilkes, J. (1977). Truth or consequences. *Child Welfare, 56*, 155–163.

Wilkes, J. (1992). Children in limbo: Working for the best outcome when children are taken into care. *Canada's Mental Health, 40*, 2–5.

Woolf, G.D. (1990). An outlook for foster care in the United States. *Child Welfare, 69*, 75–81.

Chapter Three
The Separation Experiences of Children in Foster Care

Although considerable evidence exists about the risks of separation of children from their families, and the importance of
relationships between children in foster care and their biological
families, little is available on how particular children in care
relate to their families, and how their workers may intervene.
Chapters Three, Four, and Five describe the separation experiences of 36 children in foster care, and the responses of their
workers and agencies. These children were part of a larger group
of 423 children and 75 workers from two urban Ontario Children's
Aid Societies (CASs).

Methodology

The goal of the larger project was to test whether workers who
were given intensive training in dealing with separation would be
more successful in preventing placement breakdown and in
returning children to their families than members of a control
group who did not receive the training. The results indicated that
training was associated with earlier reunion but not with placement breakdown [Palmer 1983]. As part of the training, workers
were asked to discuss one case in detail with their supervisors.
These discussions became the data base for the present study.

For the project, 36 foster care workers participated in
training, over two months, in the theory of separation of children
from the biological family and placement practices based on this
theory. The format and content of the training is shown in
Appendices A to D. The initial pool of workers included all
workers (N=75) who carried caseloads of children in regular

foster care in the two CASs. As the plan was to train them with their teams (six or seven workers with a common supervisor) for mutual reinforcement, the training and control groups were chosen randomly by teams, e.g., the names of the six teams in the larger agency were placed in a hat, and three were drawn to participate in training.

After the final training session, workers were given written instructions to present, in an audiotaped session with their supervisors, "a case where you have tried to implement the training received in dealing with separation.... Ideally, the cases should illustrate one or more of the points raised in the training."

The instructions briefly outlined the following points that had been covered in the training: (1) Begin helping children with their separation reactions early in the placement, rather than accepting the persistent myth that children should be given time to "settle into" their placements; (2) Express to children their own (the worker's) painful feelings about the child's separation experience; (3) Use play to elicit children's feelings (the training involved workers in a role-play in which "children" drew pictures of their families and workers used these to talk with the children about separation); (4) Follow-up on children's expressed feelings by using techniques such as paraphrasing or questioning; (5) Reassure children by normalizing or universalizing their place-ment experiences, that is, telling them that other children in care have similar feelings; (6) Tell children the truth about why they are in care; and (7) Use visits to previous placements or meetings with former workers to help children cope with pain or confusion about past disruptions in their lives.

The segments of case material quoted below are the com-ments of workers to their supervisors in the sessions, and, where indicated, their supervisors' responses. Workers were asked to describe their own interventions. The author assumed, in analyz-ing these excerpts, that the workers reported *all* their relevant interventions. Minor editing has been done for clarity and all names have been changed.

Generalizability of Findings

Each of the cases discussed below was selected by a worker to illustrate his or her interventions with a child experiencing separation problems. These findings should be relevant to other children in care of various ages and experiences. As the prior chapters on theory have shown, separation from their parents represents a major trauma for children in terms of object loss and developmental tasks. Moreover, the initial loss is often followed by further separations from carers or workers, adding to the accumulation of buried pain.

In considering the generalizability of these reports, it is important to take into account the training and experience of the social workers. As a group, the 36 workers could be expected to be fairly sensitive to separation dynamics: 55% had at least two years' experience in a child placement agency, 47% had a B.S.W. degree, and 31% had an M.S.W. degree. The workers also had 16 hours of intensive separation training at the outset of the study.

Children's Reactions to Separation

A range of children's separation reactions was identified by the 36 workers in their taped sessions, including reactions of anxiety, regression, physiological symptoms, denial of feelings, persistent attachment to rejecting or unreliable parents, rebellious behavior, delayed expression of feelings, self-blame for being in placement, and conflicting loyalties to foster and biological parents. Each excerpt below represents a sample of these reactions; additional examples are presented in the following chapters because they illuminate the workers' and supervisors' responses.

Anxiety

The importance to young children of being accompanied by parents when entering a new environment is explained by the theory of separation anxiety. Relying on this theory, one might expect that premature separation of young children from their parents may interrupt their normal development.

> Sara, 18 months, showed distress in her new foster home by excessive whining and clinging to any adult who showed affection to her. She would venture only a small distance before coming back to cling, apparently needing reassurance that the adult would not leave her. As Sara's worker said, "If you try to put her down eventually, she keeps clinging to you."

Sara's normal curiosity to explore her environment seems to have been inhibited by her excessive dependency on parent figures after separation. Exploration by young children requires a secure base from which they can venture out, experiment, and discover the nature of the world around them. For Sara, the disruption to her security appears to have interrupted the normal learning process, which could have long-term effects.

Behavioral Regression

According to Erikson's theory of developmental stages, children in anxiety-producing situations will regress to behaviors characteristic of an earlier stage in their lives.

> Crystal, three, was toilet trained before she was placed in foster care. After placement, she began to wet and soil her pants. Her worker had "a great deal of difficulty impressing on the foster mother that this is not that bad, that it is Crystal's reaction to all she has been through."

Crystal's behavioral regression is consistent with Erikson's theory and understandable to her social worker. Her foster mother, however, had difficulty accepting the interpretation that Crystal had been traumatized by the placement. This fits with the finding in the literature review that adults caring for a placed child tend to minimize the importance of separation.

Physiological Symptoms

The appearance of physical symptoms for which there seems to be no organic explanation is another sign that a child is under stress.

> Wendy, 16, had just been moved to a new foster home and was described by her worker as showing "all sorts of reactions. She's been sick, she's reacted in a hysterical way, she's had fainting spells, vomited, without any physical reason being found. She spent a week in a psychiatric ward, and the doctor felt that she had emotional problems mostly due to her past, not necessarily to this particular separation. She's had many moves in the past starting from when she was very young and she's not able to get close to people."

The coincidence of Wendy's symptoms with a change in homes supports the psychiatrist's diagnosis; it is understandable that a move might stir up buried feelings about earlier separations. There is no indication, however, that the worker anticipated this or tried to deal with Wendy's feelings before the move, nor did he try to analyze whether this move was more traumatic for her than earlier changes. In relation to the worker's statement that Wendy was unable to get close to people, her extreme distress may be a sign that she had begun to develop an attachment to someone in the home she had just left.

Denial and Fantasy

Some children react to separation by denial. They may hide or repress their feelings, or they may understate the importance of their loss.

> Ron, eight, had been abandoned by his single-parent mother who had disappeared four months previously, without explanation, and had made no contact with the agency. The

worker reported that when he "approached Ron on how he felt about [his] mother leaving, Ron said his mother didn't leave him, she had to go somewhere else and take care of some other affair…in his mind, his mother's going to come back."

Ron's assertion that his mother's absence was outside her control was probably a defense against the pain of feeling abandoned. In the absence of an explanation, he created a scenario in which his mother had a good reason for leaving him. To support this explanation, he had to block out reality, and this process seemed to spill over into his life generally.

"Ron will block everything out to the extent where he's engrossed in TV…you can call out his name and he won't respond even though you are sitting close to him. He kind of blocks you out…" The supervisor noted a general tendency for children in care to do this. "It seems the TV thing is part of that whole pattern" and the worker agreed, "It's a fantasy, something that's not reality, and Ron can get so engrossed in it that he doesn't have time to give to the hurtful reality."

Ron's worker recognized that Ron might be using fantasy to block out painful reality. This tendency is serious; it can develop into or reinforce schizoid tendencies in a child's personality as the child avoids reality and replaces it with an inner world that can be controlled and kept free from pain.

Persistent Attachment to Rejecting or Unreliable Parents

Some parents of young people in care showed little affection or concern for them, or made comments that seemed openly rejecting. Despite this, the young people continued to show their longing to be accepted by their parents.

Matt, 15, was told by his father [as paraphrased by the worker], "'I don't want to be seen as your father at this point, that is, I won't accept you back at home, but we can be friends.' Matt was ten feet off the ground! That was the best thing he could hear!" On Matt's next arranged home visit, however, his father was absent. "He was down low after that visit, saying 'What the heck am I getting here?' You know [worker's view] I thought we were getting somewhere, but now the father's done the same thing he did before."

The worker's concluding comment suggests disillusionment about working with Matt's father, and Matt himself seemed very hurt by his father's absence when he visited the home. It is unlikely, however, that Matt would be ready to give up on this relationship, judging from his joyful response earlier to the father's limited offer of "friendship."

Rebellious Behavior

Some adolescents came into care at their parents' request, because of rebellious behavior at home. A few even requested placement themselves because of family conflicts.

> Lesley, 15, began to run away from her placement after having come to the agency for foster care on her own initiative. As her worker said, "Her feelings about coming into care changed after she got into the foster home. Then a number of runs started occurring. Each time, the police or night duty worker would pick her up, then I would get involved. Her cooperation slowly started to dwindle and her attitude became, 'I don't want to cooperate with you, I don't want to talk to you.'"

The worker's comments suggest that Lesley presented initially as cooperative with the agency, then suddenly changed after placement. It is understandable that Lesley's family problems would not simply disappear after placement. If her request for admission had been an exaggerated assertion of the normal adolescent drive for autonomy, then she would transfer this conflict to the new authority figures. Alternatively, she may been escaping from a destructive family environment; in this case, any feelings of distrust or anger toward adults would also carry over into her relations with the worker and foster parents. This case supports the assertion, from the literature, that emotional separation from parents cannot be achieved by a physical move.

Rebelliousness sometimes erupted in children whose behavior over many years in care had been manageable, but who had experienced a number of placement disruptions.

> Dustin came into care at age three and experienced many placement changes. By age 17, he had developed serious behavior problems and came before the juvenile court. His worker connected his problems with the earlier separation and feelings of rejection: "Dustin has able to sit on things for ten to fourteen years...now he's just lost complete control. He has been in detention three times in three months, and has been moved to five different places in three months. He ran from all of them, was involved in two car thefts, drugs, homosexuality. Yet, up until that time he was perfect. He was going to concerts, theaters, then in the past three months everything went downhill."

During the "ten to fourteen years" when Dustin was assessed as holding back his feelings, he was in a series of foster homes and adoptive placements. As the worker said, "The last home was very rigid; they kept him really in a straight line and he ran from that. It's been downhill since." After his run, Dustin was moved to a group home to avoid further placement breakdowns; it was then that his behavior rapidly began to deteriorate.

The sudden deterioration in Dustin's behavior after the last placement breakdown can be understood in view of his history. Although he might be expected to be disturbed after experiencing a series of rejections, his last foster carers apparently kept his behavior in check. They were described as "rigid," so Dustin may have been under considerable pressure to contain himself. After the move to a group home, he would have less reason to hold back his underlying feelings, hence the sudden deterioration in his behavior.

This interpretation is supported by the following account of questions Dustin asked his worker.

> "Dustin didn't even know his mother and didn't know why he was in care. Nobody told him anything about his past." Consequently, Dustin "thought every placement break-down was because of him. Nobody bothered to tell him that some homes closed, that some parents decided they didn't want to adopt at the last minute."

This case exemplifies the need of children and adolescents in care for information about the past. The worker's comments imply his belief that more information would have prevented some of Dustin's self-blame for placement breakdowns that were outside his control.

Delayed Expression of Feelings

Dustin's case illustrated the tendency for pent-up feelings related to early separations to burst into the open when children reach adolescence. For youths who enter care much later, there may also be a dormant period before they openly express their separation feelings.

> Megan, 17, had to be moved from an agency-operated group home because it was closing. Her worker commented, "Now she is going through the whole thing about separating from her family, just blowing wide open...feelings that she's been sitting on for a year...It seems to have hit her the same as leaving her family; all of a sudden these people are leaving her and she's alone

again. They had a blowup in the house one night and everything came out...All of a sudden she feels it's happening to her again and she's got no control."

The feeling identified by the worker—that Megan felt she had no control over her life—would be particularly important to a 17-year-old. As noted in the discussion of theory, adolescents normally gain increasing control over their lives as they seek autonomy from their families. This process had been disrupted for Megan; she could not seek independence in the usual way, so it is understandable that she would feel alone and helpless.

> Lisa, 16, lived in a group home for a year before expressing feelings about being separated from her family. As her worker said, "She just 'blew' one night. It was brought on by something the other kids in the house were going through...and all Lisa's feelings are coming out, so we're dealing with them."

The worker's description that Lisa "just blew" suggests a spontaneous ignition of buried feelings, in an atmosphere where feelings were being freely expressed. Lisa's experience broadens the earlier evidence that feelings erupt in relation to moves, suggesting that another kind of upset or crisis may also act as a catalyst.

It may be significant that both Lisa and Megan "just blew" around the first anniversary of their separations from family. For those entering care in adolescence, this may be an important point for separation feelings to be tapped, just as the first anniversary of a death is important to someone who is bereaved.

Self-Blame Regarding Being in Placement

Young people like Dustin, above, were confused about why they were in care. Either they had not been told or could not accept the explanation; in the absence of other reasons, they tended to blame themselves.

Lara, 13, revealed to the worker her confusion about being admitted to care four years earlier. She recalled being placed in a foster home directly from a court hearing, and being told this placement would only be 'for the weekend.' Because "nobody told her anything for months, she was forced to draw her own conclusions...now Lara thinks it is her fault that she isn't home." Both worker and supervisor agreed that Lara's interpretation was "a very destructive explanation" for her.

Lara's reactions support the literature indicating that children need clear information about why they are in care. Someone may have talked with Lara, but she did not retain the explanation, possibly because she could not accept it. She developed her own account, in which she was at fault, although she apparently had no evidence of this. The only apparent advantage of Lara's self-blame may be the implication that she had some control over the situation that led to separation. A similar assumption of guilt is often seen in bereavement: the survivors search for evidence of their own responsibility for the death, which is partly a denial of their own powerlessness to control events that drastically change their lives.

Another issue is raised by Lara's memory of being told that her placement was to be very brief. This could be her distortion of reality. In the author's experience, however, workers sometimes try to allay children's fears by minimizing the nature of the separation. Their motive is probably to effect a smooth placement, with no upsetting feelings expressed. Unfortunately, they leave a destructive legacy to children who then have to create their own accounts.

In summary, young children showed their separation anxiety by regressing to behavior normally seen in those younger than themselves or by developing psychosomatic symptoms. Adolescents demonstrated unmet dependency needs less directly, by denial of abandonment or persistent attachment to parents who continued to reject them. Other reactions by adolescents included confusion, resentment, and feelings of helplessness. Some adolescents acted out their feelings in rebellious behavior; this often led to rejection by foster carers and serial re-placements.

Discussion

The young children discussed above showed a tendency to regress to previous developmental stages after being moved. Behaviors such as clinging and bedwetting can be distressing to caregivers; it is important that they understand that the behavior is probably connected to the child's separation experiences. In Crystal's case, the foster carer had difficulty accepting this; she apparently expected Crystal to behave "normally." Such expectations would probably increase children's anxiety, making them even more dependent on external support. They need a protective environment if they are to express their dependency and receive a comforting response.

Some children appeared to be unusually stoic about placement, possibly as a defense against feeling rejected or abandoned. Delayed reactions emerged in adolescents, who had apparently repressed their feelings for months and even years. It seemed that no one had succeeded, or perhaps even tried, to elicit these children's feelings of fear, anger, or sadness about losing their families. This fits with Steinhauer's observation that adults collude to pretend that separation is not a painful experience for children.

Delayed eruptions of disturbed feelings created crises for young people and others around them. Some of these feelings could be elicited earlier, if workers initiated discussion of separation when it took place. Otherwise, feelings were left to fester and explode later, in the developmental crises of adolescence. It is a particular advantage of early discussion that the workers who bring children into care usually know their families and the circumstances of the separation. Subsequent workers often have little notion of what really happened and cannot satisfy the child's need for information.

The children above who lacked important information about their pasts tended to blame themselves for the loss of their families and substitute families. Foster children must learn why they are in care even when workers may recoil from recounting painful or sad family experiences. Children who have little or no information may nurture fears that are worse than reality. Furthermore, children who think their own "badness" caused the separation will probably be relieved to learn about family conditions over which they had no control. Accordingly, their self-esteem should increase.

Lack of knowledge also contributes to children's sense of powerlessness. As described earlier, self-blame may be a rationalization by children to deal with their helplessness to prevent the separation. Egocentric thinking also allows them to deny their vulnerability to the continuing threat of unforeseen and uncontrollable changes in their lives. Giving them new information about the past may allow them to relinquish their assertion of having power and to express their fears about the present and future. Ideally, the worker can then reassure them that their views will be sought in present and future planning.

The case of Matt, who appeared to be truly rejected by his father, highlighted the differences between workers' and children's perceptions of parent involvement. The worker was discouraged by the father's apparent disinterest and seemed doubtful about continuing to work with him. The worker probably thought Matt's father would never be able to give Matt the affection he craved, and that continued contact would damage Matt's self-esteem. Yet Matt was overjoyed by even a small sign of friendship from his father, suggesting that he clung to a hope of being accepted as a son. If Matt stopped seeing his father, his memory of being rejected would probably remain; continued contact, however, would give him a chance to develop a different perspective on his father's limitations, as separate from Matt's own worth as a person.

Another risk of giving up an ambivalent or rejecting filial relationship is the possibility of distorted memories. If there is no ongoing opportunity for reality testing, both parents and child may suppress their unhappy memories, replacing them with an idealized view of the relationship. This can lead to pressure for a premature reunion that has little chance for success.

Rebellious behavior in adolescents was a major concern for workers. Despite initial promises of cooperation, behavior problems that began in the adolescent's own home tended to reappear in placement. This points to the value of including parents in the placement process: they can help to prepare new caregivers for disturbed behavior; their involvement also gives workers a chance to begin resolving family conflicts that may be fueling the adolescent's behavior.

In summary, the children described in this chapter needed to have their separation feelings recognized at an early point. They needed more information about why they were in care, and an opportunity to begin resolving feelings about their families.

References

Palmer, S.E. (1983). *The effects of training on CAS workers' handling of separation* (doctoral thesis, University of Toronto).

Chapter Four
Workers' Responses to Children's Separation Feelings

Introduction

This chapter continues the analysis of workers' audiotaped sessions with their supervisors, moving the focus to the workers' interventions. The cases are analyzed in terms of the workers' sensitivity and helpfulness to the children, and efforts are made to identify conditions associated with the quality of their responses.

As explained in the previous chapter, the research project provided training in separation theory and practice to workers and their supervisors. The workers and supervisors then were asked, in writing, to audiotape a supervision session in which they discussed a case illustrating their implementation of the training. In analyzing the sessions, it was assumed that workers would describe all their relevant interventions. If they did not mention an intervention, it was assumed there was none.

The workers related to their supervisors how they provided background information, encouraged openness about the children's pain, interpreted children's nonverbal reactions, responded to children's defenses, failed to respond to expressed or perceived feelings, minimized the importance of separation, used inclusive and exclusive approaches to foster care, and analyzed the worker-child relationships. It may seem that the emphasis of this analysis is on the gaps or negative aspects of workers' practice; this apparent bias, however, reflects the data available. All the information provided on the tapes that reflected either good or bad aspects of practice is discussed in this chapter and the next.

Providing Background Information

Information about Reason for Admission

As mentioned in the last chapter in the case reports of Dustin and Lara, some children in care were confused about why their parents had relinquished them, or why they were moved from one home to another. The children often assumed these moves were related to their own "badness."

Occasionally, a worker would discuss the circumstances of placement openly with a child from the beginning.

> Darryl, nine, was in care because his parents could not cope with his behavior. His father wanted Darryl to be placed and his mother was described by the worker as "obviously schizophrenic...threatening people with a knife." As the worker described Darryl's admission to care, Darryl's mother was "just totally out of it...didn't want anything to do with his admission...but in the end she said, 'Well, Darryl, do you want to go with these people or do you want to stay with me?' Of course, Darryl's response was he wanted to stay with her...In the end it was very gruesome, quite horrendous; we had to pick Darryl up and carry him and sneak him out the back door and to the car."

> Although this was an emergency admission, the worker spent time introducing Darryl to the foster home: "I sat down with Darryl and the foster parents from the start and explained exactly why he was coming into care." The supervisor asked, "And Darryl was right there? So there was no secret from anybody?" The worker reiterated, "That's right. That's true. That's something that I've been really successful in avoiding—the secrecy. I felt good in the way

that we handled this case—there are no secrets from Darryl!" The worker also told the foster carers from the beginning that Darryl did not want to be with them, that he "didn't want any part of foster care."

The references to secrecy, by both the supervisor and worker, suggest their shared recognition that to avoid discussing the reason for admission with children and foster carers is the usual approach. In a case like this, some workers would have difficulty telling foster carers about Darryl's mother's mental illness, his father's negative attitude, and Darryl's difficult behavior, especially in Darryl's presence. It might also be difficult for Darryl to tell the foster carers he objected to the admission, if the worker had not revealed this. Subsequent to this open discussion, Darryl was able to make his need for family contact known to the worker.

> "Separation is something that Darryl raises all the time...we discuss the whole matter of why he's not with his parents...at first he was very demanding, very persistent, very pushy about, 'When am I going to see my parents?'...he threatened to get a lawyer...now it's changed because he knows the visits are on a regular basis, and will only be canceled if the parents back out...he's started to trust me...and beginning to trust the world."

Only two workers in the study reported talking with a child about the reason for admission to care, and only one held this discussion in conjunction with foster carers. The model portrayed in the project training included children, parents, and foster carers discussing the placement together, but no worker reported using this model.

Information to Reduce Confusion

Some young people had been placed in care many years earlier, but only began to question their workers in adolescence. Two workers described their attempts to fill gaps in the children's knowledge of their earlier years.

> Troy, 15, was back in agency care because his adoption had broken down. He asked his worker many questions about his early life. As the worker said, "These are questions that children in their own homes can easily have answered by their parents...questions such as, 'How much did I weigh when I was born? What did I look like?'" There was some information in the agency file, but the worker was unsure how much of it was confidential. He said, "I was writing something down and I looked up and he's going through his file and he's looking at it. I said, 'Troy, you're not supposed to look at it.' 'Well, why not? It's all about me, why shouldn't I look at it?' I was willing to say, 'Okay, go ahead, do it.' Then I thought, 'My God, he's not supposed to do this.'"

> The worker went on to note that "Troy is someone who could really use some background information because I'm sure that right now the reason why the adoption broke down was because he didn't give the family a chance. He had a wall built up when he was about seven years old, when he came into care, and it's still there now and I still think he needs to deal with the past." As a result, the worker decided to go through the case record with Troy, discussing sequentially each unsuccessful placement, and helping him to walk back through these homes in his mind. The worker explored with him why each placement had ended and dealt with the feelings these memories aroused in Troy.

Troy's concern about his past may have existed for years, and emerged only in adolescence, when his identity became a pressing issue. He certainly did not recall being told anything about the past. The worker's dilemma illustrates a conflict between bureaucratic demands to withhold information from clients, and professional imperatives to respond to an adolescent's need to know about his history. Troy's worker responded to his expressed need, but this was the only time a worker mentioned sharing agency records with a child.

Information to Minimize Self-Blame

In the other case of a worker providing background information, the reason for the family breakup was the mother's chronic mental illness combined with the father's inability to cope alone. These circumstances would probably be easier to explain to a child than events involving parental neglect or abuse.

> Lindsay, 14, began to question his worker about his father, who left the family when Lindsay was four. The worker was able to tell him, "Well at one point when your mother was in the hospital your father took care of all of you, then it just got to be too much." This was a valuable revelation by the worker: "It meant everything to Lindsay to know that his father had tried for a little while before he deserted the whole situation."

The agency was apparently the only source for this information, as Lindsay's father had never returned to the family. Lindsay's positive reaction to new information about his family suggests that he may have previously concluded that his father had no interest in caring for him. His self-esteem would be raised by learning that his mother had been hospitalized and his father had tried to keep him and his siblings, placing them only as a last resort. This knowledge might also facilitate Lindsay's development of an autonomous identity: as described earlier, part of a child's identity is formed by internalizing positively viewed parental characteristics. Thus, children have a basis for better identity formation if they are aware of characteristics they can value in their parents. Upon learning his history, Lindsay would be able to identify with a father who had tried to care for him, rather than simply abandoning him as Lindsay might previously have thought.

"Socially Desirable" Explanations

Rather than giving children truthful answers that might be painful, workers sometimes gave them socially desirable reasons why they could not remain in their own homes.

> Cathy, three, and Susan, 18 months, were sisters whose mother left the family suddenly, without explanation. Their father initially placed them in a small children's institution, but made no attempt to keep in touch with them. After a few weeks, CAS was drawn in and the girls were moved to a foster home. When Cathy asked the worker about her father's absence, she was told that he had to work. She rejected this explanation, saying, "My Daddy does not work! I want to go to my Daddy!" The worker reassured her supervisor that "she must have believed me because she stopped asking by the time we got to the foster home."

Another explanation for Cathy to have "stopped asking" is that she may have lost hope of receiving a truthful answer. The worker, however, seems to be inferring from her silence a lack of interest in her father: Cathy's feelings were not mentioned again, nor was any initiative taken to encourage visiting. Visits with the father did not begin for a month after placement in the foster home. Socially desirable responses were also given when Cathy questioned both the worker and her grandmother about her mother's absence. Each of them gave a different explanation.

> According to the worker, "I said her Mom had gone away on a trip and we didn't know when she would be back. At the same time, the grandmother was saying that her Mommy was sick in the hospital. According to the foster mother, Cathy is having a great deal of difficulty accepting that her

mother is away." The worker went on to say that Cathy "is getting two messages so it is no wonder she is getting confused." She also criticized the grandmother's story as not being "totally honest."

Despite her recognition that Cathy was confused, the worker did not try to clarify the contradiction for Cathy, nor did she seem to be aware that, like the grandmother, she had given an explanation that was not "totally honest." From Cathy's viewpoint, the explanation that her mother had left for a trip, apparently willingly and without saying good-bye, might be more painful than the truth—that no one knew where her mother was. While the latter explanation might cause anxiety, the explanation of a planned trip is more likely to be viewed as a rejection by Cathy; it suggests that her mother wanted to leave and did not care enough to explain this to her.

In the author's experience, children are often told that parents are "working," "have to go away," or "have to go to the hospital." The last reason may be understandable to a child whose parent is physically ill, but frequently the hospitalization is psychiatric. In this case, a young child, who associates hospitals with physical illness, requires a complete explanation for a hospitalization. Usually the child has experienced a deterioration in the parent's behavior, so reference can be made to this as a condition requiring a doctor's care. Another advantage of a full and truthful explanation is that it leads to greater consistency in the responses given to a child's queries by the various adults involved.

Encouraging Openness about Children's Pain

In two cases, children were encouraged to express their feelings about the separation at the time it was happening.

Maria, eight, and Rocco, five, had to be admitted to care when their mother entered a psychiatric hospital. Their father and grandmother were involved in the admission, although the children had been living alone with their mother; they knew the worker, who had been visiting their home for about six months because of their mother's erratic functioning. After making plans with the adults alone, the worker then included the children, encouraging the father and grandmother to prepare them for foster care: "I told them I was there because their grandmother was concerned that they didn't have a place to stay. I made sure they knew their mother was in hospital, then I asked the father and the grandmother to tell the children about the placement and they did."

"I explained the meaning of a foster home. The children both began to cry, not loudly, not out of control. Rocco clung to his father and Maria clung to her grandmother. Maria said, 'I want to stay with grandma,' and Rocco said he wanted to stay with his father, but the adults felt they could not take the children. The grandmother began to say, 'There'll be a nice home, lots of kids and a dog and a cat and dolls and new toys.' I was more realistic, telling Maria and Rocco we really didn't know yet which home they'd be in. I told them it was all right to be angry and to cry if they wanted to. It seemed at that point there were no secrets anymore, the kids knew everything. That was the point where they seemed relaxed; when I left a short time later, they both said 'Bye, we'll see you.'"

The worker's encouragement opened the way for the children to express their separation feelings to their father and grandmother. Although their crying and clinging were undoubtedly painful for everyone concerned, it was supportive to Maria and Rocco to share their feelings openly with their father and grandmother. The worker also normalized their possible anger, which would make it easier for them to express it then or later. In view of the internal conflicts of children in care described in the literature review, the expression of anger would be a healthy reaction to the psychological assault of separation.

In another case, the sensitive response came from a foster carer, Mrs. P., who had requested that a child be moved from her home; apparently, her extended family in another city needed her. Mrs. P. had herself experienced placement in childhood, as had her husband.

> Andy, seven, was moved to a new home by Mrs. P. because his worker was ill. The worker explained that "once they got to the new place, Mrs. P. introduced Andy to the new foster parents, then sat down with him and was quite supportive. She encouraged Andy to talk, saying 'Well, you weren't with us very long and you're going somewhere else and it's okay to be sad. What are you feeling?' When it was time for Mrs. P. to leave the new home, Andy ran up to her and he put his arms around her, saying 'Can you stay a little longer?' She did. She felt bad about leaving him, but realistically that's what you've got to do."

In discussing Mrs. P.'s sensitivity with her, the worker noted that Andy was Mrs. P.'s first foster child and she had not been given any instruction about supporting children during a move. According to the worker, Mrs. P. explained her responsiveness in terms of "she felt that if she were Andy she would want someone around that she could talk to."

Mrs. P.'s empathy with Andy may well have come from her own experience in foster care; this would enable her to identify with Andy and give him the support she herself had once needed. This illustration suggests that insight into feelings about personal separation experiences might be an asset to workers in helping children. It may also have helped that this was Mrs. P.'s first experience as a foster carer; she might have been less defended against discussing separation than experienced foster carers who might guard against their own sense of loss in parting with children.

Responding to Defensiveness

Workers' Frustration with Adolescent Denial of Feelings

Separation feelings often became accessible only during a crisis, such as a placement change.

> Mike, 16, was described by his worker as "arrogant...which is why he is having to move...presenting himself as perfect...saying [in relation to the foster home], 'I'll live my own life, I'll be home by curfew so what's the big hassle?' All he's doing is sleeping and eating there and the foster parents naturally want more for their involvement than that..." The worker recounted how he "kept after Mike, trying to get him to talk about his parents, yet Mike always closed it off very quickly. Yet Mike began to cry when the worker told him he had to move to a new home. As the worker recounted, "He felt the feelings that I guess he hasn't felt for some time. So with a lot of these kids, it's just in the time of a crisis that they'll start to bring out their feelings. In between times you could hit them with a sledgehammer and they're just so tight and perfect that they won't get into it at all."

Mike's worker showed sensitivity by linking Mike's fears about the move to possible buried feelings about past moves. Yet his final statement, referring to hitting children "with a sledge-hammer," suggests that he had abandoned traditional skills for eliciting children's feelings and was showing his frustration with their defensiveness. He might have been reacting subjectively to the separation experiences of Mike and others, identifying with them, or perhaps feeling uncomfortable about his role in separating families.

Acceptance of Defenses at Face Value

Workers sometimes accepted children's presenting attitudes about separation as valid. When these children's subsequent behaviors were inconsistent with their professed attitudes, the workers were puzzled, but did not seem to reconsider their initial assessment.

Alison, 15, came to CAS attention because she was out of her mother's control. She made an agreement with the worker to move into an agency group home. According to the worker, "Alison liked the idea and was looking forward to the group home. She said she had spoken to other girls who had been in a group home and it sounded good to her." Before the move could be made, however, Alison began a pattern of running away from home.

According to the worker, "After that interview [when she and Alison discussed moving to the group home] I was never in touch with Alison. She would run from home and be missing for a week, then she would return for about a day and a half. On the last return, her mother called to let me know that Alison was home but just as the mother and I were setting a time to meet, Alison left to go on an errand, and did not return." The placement was finally done eight days later, when the agency's night duty worker was called to Alison's home and took her to the foster home, handling the situation as an emergency. There was no mention of anyone discussing Alison's feelings with her, either then or later.

Despite Alison's running behavior, the worker did not view her as anxious about placement; she commented about the eventual admission that Alison "was very nonchalant about the whole process. She didn't seem concerned at all. She did not want to go back home anyway. She seemed okay about coming into care."

The worker's assessment is inconsistent with Alison's running behavior: the timing of its onset, just after she agreed to come into care, suggests that her nonchalant attitude was probably a cover for anxiety about moving to an unknown home. Because the worker assumed that Alison's presenting attitude of wanting placement was a true reflection of her feelings, the worker failed to handle Alison's apparent ambivalence about the placement. Thus she missed an opportunity to reach Alison at a feeling level, leaving her to deal with her feelings by running away.

When adolescents take the initiative and request placement in foster care, workers may wrongly assume they have no ambivalent feelings about their decision.

> Lesley, 15, mentioned in the previous chapter, was running away continually from her placement. The supervisor asked her worker, "Do you think Lesley is upset about being in care?" Initially, the worker said, "No, I don't get that feeling at all. She came into the office willingly to request her own placement." The worker's next comments, however, seem to contradict her initial assessment: "Her feelings about coming into care changed after she got into the foster home. Then a number of runs took place [usually to a friend's home]. Each time [alerted by the foster carers] the police or night duty worker would pick her up, then I would get involved. Her cooperation slowly started to dwindle and her attitude became, 'I don't want to cooperate with you, I don't want to talk to you.'"

The worker's denial that Lesley might be upset about being in care, followed by contradictory information, suggests some resistance to analyzing Lesley's feelings and to engaging her at a deeper level. The resistance might arise from frustration: the worker had accepted Lesley's request for placement as legitimate, and had assumed official responsibility for her through the agency. Now she was being harassed by worrisome behavior and a rejecting attitude from Lesley. For the worker to agree with her supervisor that Lesley might have some negative reactions to being in care would seem to be acknowledging that the decision for placement had been approached superficially. With encouragement from the supervisor, the worker might have explored the inconsistencies in her analysis, but there was no further discussion in this session.

Failing to Respond to Expressed or Perceived Feelings

Unexplained Nonresponse

Some workers reported the children's feelings of anxiety or self-blame, but mentioned no attempt by themselves to explore or otherwise respond to these feelings. This is not conclusive evidence of their nonintervention, but the inference is reasonable: the instructions for the audiotaped reports were given to all workers and supervisors, asking them to discuss the worker's handling of separation in terms of the training they had received.

> Apparent failure to intervene was seen with both Megan and Lara, who were discussed in Chapter Three. Megan's worker showed empathy with her panic about having to leave yet another home, but gave no indication that she planned to help Megan with these feelings. The worker and supervisor responsible for Lara agreed that her self-blame about the placement was "a very destructive explanation"; but they gave no indication that they intended to help Lara with it.

In these two cases, the workers and supervisors expressed concern about children's separation feelings, but did not take the next step of trying to help them understand and accept their past. Considering that responding to expressed feelings is basic to social work intervention, it seems that the workers were unusually passive. Probably the same dynamics were operating in these instances as discussed earlier, that is, workers were sensitive to children's feelings but apparently failed to act on their understanding. Most of these workers had professional training in social work, as well as the special training in separation provided by the project, yet they did not seem to use their skills to help the children with their separation reactions. The workers may have been overburdened, defending against their own feelings, or fearful of eliciting reactions that might upset a placement.

Impediments to Exploring Children's Feelings

Although most workers gave no reason why they did not deal with the children's separation reactions, two workers did mention external impediments to doing so: uncooperative parents and language barriers.

Parents understandably become anxious and sometimes angry during the legal process of having their children taken into care. When the admission comes about because of out-of-control behavior on the part of their child, the parents' resentment may be projected onto the child.

> Casey, 13, was readmitted to care at his parents' request, and the worker reported that "Casey was upset and angry at his parents. When I discussed the reasons for readmission, he attempted to display a cool attitude of not caring about the rejection by his parents, but his nonverbal behavior indicated that he was very unhappy, anxious almost to the point of being overwrought. He was close to tears on several occasions during our discussion. His fists were clenched, his whole body was tight. He was definitely very upset."

By initiating discussion of the separation, the worker brought Casey's feelings very close to the surface. He showed sensitivity by noting that Casey was close to tears and very tense, and by recognizing that Casey's cool attitude was a defense. He could have probed a little for Casey's barely concealed feelings in the above interview, but at least he began the process. Having opened the subject, he could use this experience as a basis for reaching Casey's feelings in later interviews.

The supervisor asked, "Were you able to involve the parents...in helping the boy understand why he was placed back into care?" The worker explained, "The parents, Casey, and I spoke briefly at court but the parents were so hostile to Casey, before and during the court hearing, that they were very reluctant to speak with him at all or discuss the issue. They were quite defensive about the whole thing."

It is understandable that the worker may have wished to protect Casey from a hostile discussion in which he might be further rejected by his parents. As there was no further mention of the subject, however, the impression is left that Casey was given no explanation for his readmission. Lacking an explanation, Casey would be likely to imagine the worst—that he was totally at fault in the situation.

Another worker was inhibited from dealing with feelings by a language barrier between herself and the child's mother.

Gino, eight, was admitted to care with his four younger siblings, "following an assault by his mother on him, his brother, and two sisters." The supervisor asked the worker, "Did the mother respond to the children's feelings to prepare them for the move?" and the worker responded, "No, she didn't. There was a considerable language problem [presumably between the mother and worker] and I didn't ask her to."

A further question from the supervisor about separation reactions elicited from the worker a general negation that Gino was upset or needed support through the move: "Oh, although he was injured he didn't complain about his injury. Neither has he asked any questions about how long he will be in care or where he'll be living. He's relieved that he is going to be placed with his brother but he doesn't seem unduly concerned that his other three siblings are not going to be in the same home...I feel that he trusts me."

The supervisor again tried to find out what the worker actually said to Gino: "During the actual drive to the foster home did you engage in any discussion of his feelings about what was happening?" and the worker explained, "I prepared him for what was going to happen while we were still at the hospital, but it was actually a night duty worker who drove him to the emergency placement."

As gradually revealed by this account, Gino was taken from his own home and placed, without preparation, into an unfamiliar home, by someone he did not know. Lack of casework help is common in emergency placements. The disturbing element in this instance is the worker's apparent belief that the work done with Gino was adequate to meet his needs. She implied that Gino's apparent lack of concern about admission to care was attributable to his "trust" in her, yet it is unlikely that trust in a worker would eliminate a child's anxiety in a such a traumatic situation. It seems more probable that Gino repressed his anxiety about the separation. Because of the language barrier, the worker did not try to have Gino's mother prepare the children for separation. She could have sought someone to interpret, even Gino himself, if she believed in the value of including the mother in the placement process. The worker may have been using the language difference to rationalize her position, because she was reluctant to deal with painful feelings.

Workers' Hesitance to Elicit Painful Feelings

Workers often lack the knowledge and skills necessary for responding to foster children's separation conflicts. Occasionally, workers expressed their sense of inadequacy; they were aware of children's needs, but were not confident about discussing separation.

Mark, nine, was reported by his worker as needing to express his "very pent-up, very repressed" feelings about his separation experience. She said, "I think he's letting go of his old illusions, but he's still repressing all his feelings because they are extremely painful and dangerous." The worker expressed self-doubt about her ability to help Mark with his feelings: "In terms of nonverbal communication, I haven't done too much myself...I haven't done very much play therapy or role-playing." Consequently, she took the role of an observer, saying, "I really haven't intervened with Mark, but I'm sort of picking up the cues."

This worker was clearly sensitive to Mark's separation feelings, but felt too unsure of herself to engage with him at this level.

Another worker expressed similar uncertainty about discussing a child's "missing" mother with him.

Ron, eight, did not mention his mother to his worker for several months after his admission to care. The worker reported, "I find I'm conscious of when to mention 'mother' and in what context. Should I arrange a visit or wait for the court hearing? How does he feel about his mother leaving him? Does he realize his mother has left him? These are the kind of questions I'm asking myself about how to pose the subject to him."

These two workers were open about their discomfort, implicitly seeking direction from their supervisors; with encouragement and guidance, they might have been able to approach the children's feelings. Their supervisors did not respond to their expressions of concern, however, which suggests that knowledge and skill may also have been lacking at the supervisory level.

Minimizing the Importance of Separation

There was some evidence that workers minimized the effects on children of changing workers or homes, particularly when the change was caused by organizational structures. In agencies that were organized by specialized functions, the child's worker tended to change at the point of admission to care, or when the child's relationship to the agency changed from short term to long term. In agencies where workers were assigned to foster homes, rather than to children, a child who had to move often lost a familiar worker in the process. Finally, some agencies purposely placed children into short-term homes for a few weeks before making long-term placements; this gave the workers time to seek an appropriate home, but the move might feel like another rejection to the child.

The following cases illustrate the attitudes of workers and supervisors toward organizationally caused changes for children.

> John, eight, and his sister Jennifer, six, experienced two changes of workers within a short time period because of agency structures related to specialization. The children were transferred from the family worker who brought them into care to a children's worker; then the latter worker made a decision to leave the agency, just as John and Jennifer were about to move from a temporary to a somewhat more permanent home. The departing worker, in discussing these changes with her supervisor, minimized the potential harm to the children, saying "I don't see a big problem with them. They are almost used to going from place to place."

> After downplaying the potential effect of these changes on John and Jennifer, the worker went on to express concern about the effects of the move on the foster carers. She told her supervisor that the present foster carers had unresolved feelings about the pending move: "Maybe it does far more to the adults than it does to the children," and the supervisor agreed, "Exactly."

The worker and supervisor appear to be minimizing the disruptive effects on foster children of having to change homes and workers, in agreeing that their imminent move would be easier for them than for the foster carers they were leaving. Their analysis contradicts accepted knowledge about the devastating effects of moving children from one home to another.

Another worker exemplified this tendency to show more empathy for adults than for children who were facing separation.

> "My first thought when I came to work here was that the parents should not be asked to go to the foster home at the time of placement. I thought, 'Boy, that would be a really bad experience for the parent to have to go along and go through all of this....to feel bad about putting this kid in a foster home...having to meet that lady who's going to take over their role and the whole bit.'"

This worker did not contend that an adult's pain might be greater than a child's, but his focus on parents' feelings could be detrimental to the children he placed, as it may deter him from asking parents to accompany their children on a move.

The tendency to give priority to the feelings of foster carers or to parents probably derives from several sources. Adults have the maturity, lacking in children, to give verbal expression to their feelings; similarly, workers find it easier to identify with adults, by imagining themselves in a similar situation. Priorities are also influenced by relative power. Foster carers have more power than parents, who have more power than children; consequently, workers may feel pressed to think of their needs in that order. In effect, the priority accorded to the needs of these three groups may be inversely related to their vulnerability.

Using Inclusive/Exclusive Approaches to Foster Care

Including Families in Admission to Care

The inclusion of children's families in the admission to care was reported by only two workers. The first case was Maria and Rocco, mentioned earlier; the second was Tom, who is discussed in the subsequent section.

Maria, eight, and Rocco, five, were accompanied to the new home by their grandmother, although their father "could not" come. The worker noted: "The kids seemed happy and didn't appear to be upset. On the way I tried to explain where we were going and what it would be like. I had called the foster mother and explained that I was going to be honest with the children, that I didn't want to sugarcoat this experience for them; I said it was important that the children be allowed to feel their pain."

"When we arrived, the foster mother was quite helpful in making the children and the grandmother feel at home. We all talked for a while, got acquainted in the living room...I suggested that perhaps Maria and Rocco see their bedroom first and then they could go out and play. They decided they wanted to do that...marched upstairs and spent some time in their room, looking at where they'd be staying. After about an hour, they seemed to settle right in. They were both very comfortable and they wanted to go out and play. The grandmother and I left."

The worker had already laid the groundwork by allowing Maria and Rocco to express their sadness about leaving home. A preplacement visit would have been the ideal next step, but the presence of their grandmother during the move seems to have given them comfort. Their manner of "marching" to the new bedroom and their readiness to "go out and play" suggests they were accepting the move at least at a superficial level.

Awareness of Value of Parental Accompaniment

Tom's case was one of the few where the worker managed to provide a preplacement visit; furthermore, Tom's father accompanied him on the visit.

Tom, six, was accompanied by his father when his worker took him to visit his prospective foster home. The worker described the insight he gained into Tom's behavior by imagining himself in Tom's place: "I put myself in his shoes, having visited unfamiliar people with my parents as a child; it had been very comforting to know that my father was in the front room talking to the people. In that way I would be able to do whatever I wanted...go out and play with the other kids and get to know them. I think that [having Tom's father there] was a source of comfort to Tom."

This worker was clearly focused on the child's needs, and could identify with Tom by recalling his own childhood experiences. This case suggests that workers can gain insight into children's separation anxiety by drawing from their own early experiences in ordinary situations. This worker seemed to be quite open to considering Tom's feelings and examining his own personal reactions. It may be significant that the worker was new to the agency when the separation project began.

Although the concept of inclusiveness is theoretically accepted in child welfare, only two of the 36 workers (Maria and Rocco's worker, and Tom's worker) reported arranging for relatives to accompany children on the first visit to an unfamiliar home. Furthermore, Tom was the only child in the study who was given a preplacement visit. It is probably significant that Tom's worker was new to the agency at the time the project began; thus, he was given training in the concept of inclusiveness before being exposed to customary agency placement practices.

Using Separation Theory in Assessment

One worker used the concept of inclusiveness to interpret a child's problems and formulate an intervention.

Ron, eight, was having problems in school and his foster mother [a special education teacher] felt he had an attention deficit regarding homework. The worker reported that Ron would become engrossed in television to the point of "blocking everything out. You can call out his name and he won't respond, even though you are sitting right next to him."

The worker attributed these problems to Ron's concern about his mother, who had disappeared several months earlier. He said, "Well, perhaps after you've gone and talked to your mother you'll be able to concentrate more on your work; now you're spending so much time thinking about your mother that you can't spell words correctly or you're too busy involved with television."

The worker showed insight into separation dynamics by interpreting Ron's school problems and absorption with television as related to his mother's disappearance. Furthermore, the worker's comments gave Ron recognition of his feelings and an invitation to express them.

Unrealistic Expectations for Attachment

Theory suggests that children who lack a trusting relationship with their parents will have difficulty in trusting other parent figures. In this light, some workers held unrealistic expectations for children to form new attachments.

Dominic, 15, was reported as being completely rejected by his father. As the worker said, "The father removed himself and said he wanted nothing further to do with Dominic. He wouldn't support him, he wouldn't see him, he wouldn't help me plan anything for his son, wouldn't even come to court. And Dominic—I think, to protect himself—was doing the same thing back. I guess I'm thinking maybe we could link him up with people almost similar to his own, in some respect...some of their qualities anyway...there were a lot of things he liked about his father, so I thought, 'In some respects, any father figure may be accepted by this boy.' He seems to feel some comfort toward men in general."

The worker's assessment of Dominic as eager for acceptance

by a father figure seems to be justified, but his "comfort toward men in general" is hardly likely to outweigh the effects of being rejected by his father. Before Dominic could form a trusting relationship with another father figure, he would have to work through this rejection, to see it as a relationship problem rather than a result of his own inadequacy. By seeking immediately to replace Dominic's father with "any father figure," the worker seems to be engaging in wishful thinking, and may be setting Dominic up for further disappointment.

The tendency to have unrealistic expectations for children to relate to substitute parents was discussed by another worker and supervisor.

> The supervisor said, "I think [the difficulties encountered in placement] are understandable because we put these kids into these homes and we say, 'Bond to this person...to this thing...you become part of it' and then we pull them away." The worker agreed, "We say 'Bond to somebody new' and, even at age five or seven, they are too old to do this."

The casual way that some workers use the term "bonding" was also exemplified in relation to Casey, mentioned earlier. Although Casey showed hurt and anger about being rejected by his parents only a few months earlier, his worker suggested, "at this point it's in Casey's best interest to bond with the new foster family." The term "bond" seems to be misused in these discussions. Bonding can be defined as a profound attachment, such as develops in a trusting relationship between infants and their parents. In this sense, children who have been moved to unfamiliar homes, usually under circumstances of deprivation or conflict, are poor candidates to bond with new parent figures. Bonding is a particularly remote possibility for an older child, like Dominic, who has been recently rejected by a parent. Workers' use of the term in such cases may reflect a simple misunderstanding of the term; it may also be viewed as a denial of the damage done to children by their experiences with rejection and/or inadequate parenting.

Ignoring Importance of Family

A worker who was unsuccessful in eliciting separation feelings from a boy who said he wanted to be admitted to care concluded that the youth had no ambivalence about being in care.

> Robert, 12, was admitted to care as an emergency, after having been charged as a young offender. His mother wanted the admission because she was afraid he would get into "serious trouble"; she was "quite negative" and "basically wanted him and his brother out." Robert was seen by his worker as having no anxiety about being admitted to care. The worker commented, "I tried to get at some of his feelings about not returning home. He did not appear to me to be anxious about leaving home; rather he was quite pleased and looked forward to going into an emergency bed."
>
> The supervisor questioned the worker's assessment. "So you didn't find that this was only the surface of a very traumatic situation?" The worker was very definite: "No, I did not. This was something he was asking for some time beforehand; finally it was happening and he was quite content to leave his mother and go into another home." The supervisor asked whether Robert might have some postplacement regrets, "now that he has been in care for some time and hasn't returned home?" This time the worker was more dogmatic, even commenting on Robert's *thoughts*: "No, he has not. He is looking forward to remaining in care. He is not looking forward to going back home. He doesn't *think* about going back home. He wants to remain in care. He is quite pleased." [emphasis added]

Possibly the worker was right about Robert's feelings: undoubtedly many children experience some relief upon coming into care, particularly if they have been living in a neglectful or abusive home situation. Theoretically, it can be anticipated that Robert would feel ambivalent about being in care. Even if correct, however, the worker's claim to know Robert's *thoughts* suggests that he is protesting too much; no one has access to another's unspoken thoughts. The worker may be taking this position as a defense against the supervisor's doubts rather than from a thoughtful consideration of Robert's situation.

Worker-Child Relationships as An Aspect of Separation

Workers' Emphasis on Own Importance vs. Importance of Child's Family

Occasionally, workers behaved as though they believed children were more interested in them than in their families. In the case of Maria and Rocco, described earlier, the worker was sensitive and inclusive throughout the admission until the point of saying good-bye to the children in the foster home.

> After inviting Maria and Rocco to express their sadness and anger about separation, and taking their grandmother with them to the foster home, the worker seemed to revert to a more traditional stance in the final stage of placement. He said, "When the grandmother and I left, I told the kids I'd be back to see them regularly. They gave their grandmother a big hug, they gave me a big hug and a kiss." He did tell the children their parents would be allowed to visit, but he told the supervisor they would probably not be reliable, saying, "I think the bottom line for these kids, as far as visiting goes, is that I said I'd be back in a few days and that I'd visit them regularly."

The worker's attention to his own relationship with the children, leaving family visits unsettled, carries the implication that he is more important to the children than their family members. Certainly, he has temporarily assumed responsibility for them, but he cannot emotionally replace their parents.

Another worker seemed to offer himself and the agency as

consolation to a boy whose mother had abandoned him several months before.

> Ron, eight, discussed earlier, had been abandoned four months earlier by his single-parent mother. The worker reported Ron questioning him: "Have I made attempts to look for her? What attempts have I made?" and that the feeling behind these questions seemed "very despondent."

> The worker responded to Ron's hopes for reunion with his mother by expressing the agency's doubts about his mother's suitability to care for him: "If your mother comes back, we don't know if it will be a good idea for her to have you back; so we're going to let the judge decide." Apparently the worker did not seek Ron's reaction to this possibility. The supervisor then suggested that Ron's unrealistic hopes of reunion with his mother had to be confronted: "It's time we zeroed in and said 'Look Ron, this is the reality and you've got to face it.'" The worker felt he had tried to do this at Christmas, just after Ron came into care, saying, "Why hasn't your mother been around or why hasn't she even given you a gift? We have, we care; this means we care."

Confronting Ron with his mother's neglect of him seems insensitive to Ron's feelings. His persistent hope for his mother's return is probably Ron's defense against the insecurity of an unknown future; it is unlikely he would abandon this hope without an acceptable alternative. The worker offered the agency's demonstrated care to Ron as a replacement for his mother, yet separation theory indicates that the parents cannot be so easily replaced. By comparing Ron's mother unfavorably with the agency, the worker implied that Ron would benefit by concluding that his mother did not care about him. Ron might eventually reach this conclusion himself but, at age eight, such a view could be devastating to his self-image. His persistent hope for his mother's return would provide a defense against feeling rejected and having to face the loss of his only remaining parent. The worker showed a laudable desire to help Ron with his feelings, but the stark confrontation he described is only likely to reinforce Ron's defenses.

The worker's apparent insensitivity may arise from personal pain generated by an identification with Ron in his bleak situation, in the manner suggested by Steinhauer. Ron's persistent longing for his mother seemed to frustrate the worker: possibly he felt sad that he could not produce the mother, angry with her for abandoning her son, and even irritated with Ron for not valuing the agency's attempts to compensate him for the loss. The worker's response seems geared to his personal agenda rather than to Ron's needs. In addition to the risk of hurting Ron, the worker may pass his anger toward the mother on to the foster carers. It is important for workers to be aware of their negative feelings toward parents so that these feelings do not insidiously affect how they and others treat the child.

Special Worker-Child Relationships

About 20% of the children in this study had no contacts with any relatives. It is not known how many of these children had strong attachments to their foster carers, but a few adolescents were described by their workers as being isolated from any family connections.

> The worker for Peter, 16, said: "Peter doesn't know what a relationship is. I'm the only person he has. That's sad, to have a social worker for your only relationship."

> The primary attachment of Jamie, 18, also seemed to be to his worker. The worker had placed him in care in his early teens, at the beginning of her child welfare experience, and he continued to telephone her after leaving care. "I think I became very significant to him because I was with him through this difficult time. He's been in and out of jail. He's not doing so well. He was the first kid with whom I ever

worked, and he still calls me up and lets me know 'where he's at.' He remembers me as one significant person who didn't reject him no matter what he did. I hung in there and he remembers that."

The worker attributed Jamie's attachment partly to her involvement in his original placement. It is understandable that children who lose touch with their families may place great significance on the worker who knew them and took part in the original separation. This illustrates the importance of maintaining continuity of workers, and eliminating bureaucratic structures that interfere with this, such as changing workers when children move from short-term to long-term care.

The worker also attributed Jamie's attachment to her continuing acceptance of him. The quality of unconditional acceptance, however, is supposed to be part of all social work relationships. It may be most important that Jamie was the first child the worker had taken into care. The responsibility for separating a child from his family would probably have a great impact on a beginning worker, involving a deep investment of emotion, and creating an attachment to the child. Accordingly, Jamie may have responded to the worker's attachment to him. This is not likely to happen often, as most workers do not have the emotional energy to become attached to every child they place. It is notable that Maria and Rocco's worker, who handled their preparation for placement with unusual sensitivity, was also in his first few months with the agency. He was oriented to inclusiveness by the workshop on separation provided by this project; otherwise, as he said, "I probably wouldn't have considered asking the father or grandmother to come along with me to the placement."

Discussion

A sizable minority of the workers demonstrated sensitivity to children's explicit reactions to separation, and some workers identified separation problems that were indirectly expressed, but few intervened in ways consistent with separation theory and placement principles. Rarely did workers include parents in the separation process or actively elicit a child's painful feelings, and only a few gave children information about the past, encouraged their expression of feelings, or practiced inclusiveness. More often, workers seemed to overlook the importance of separation or were deterred, for various reasons, from dealing with it.

The following discussion examines children's responses to workers' positive interventions, as well as conditions associated with responsiveness and unresponsiveness in workers.

Beneficial Effects of Providing Background Information

The findings support the value of giving children information about their past experiences and why they are in care. After Darryl's worker spoke plainly with him and the foster carers about the reason for placement, Darryl was able to be open about his separation reactions. Troy's worker reported, after letting him read his history with the agency, that Troy "could really use some background information." Lindsay's worker said "it meant everything to Lindsay" to know that his father had initially tried to care for him.

These adolescents were given information that could counter a sense of being "kidnapped" by the agency, of having no history, or of having been carelessly or intentionally abandoned by their parents. Such information can modify feelings of anger, confusion, or low self-esteem. Background information also makes it easier for children to discuss the past with their parents, foster carers, and workers. Through discussion, they can begin to develop a reality-based account of their separations and eventually come to terms with the past.

Only Troy's and Lindsay's workers reported giving children information about their past. As suggested above, the other workers may have been afraid of upsetting children by discussing family problems prior to placement, or they may have been avoiding pain for themselves.

Notably, Troy and Lindsay seem to have held back their questions about separation from their families until adolescence. As they reached the stage when most young people seek independence from their families, their need for self-knowledge seems to have overcome their fear of hearing painful news. Whatever the reason, their questions indicate large gaps in their knowledge about themselves. This suggests that workers taking over responsibility for a child at any age cannot assume that previous workers have filled in the gaps; all workers should give background information routinely to all children on their caseloads.

Value of Including Families and Being Open about Pain

When workers involve family members in placement and acknowledge that separation from families is painful, children have a chance to express feelings that would otherwise be suppressed and to be comforted by people they trust. Maria and Rocco were able to show their sadness and to reach out for comfort, as they cried and clung to their grandmother and father. Andy's foster carer showed she understood it was hard for him to move, and he subsequently asked her to stay longer with him at the new home. After seeking and receiving reassurances, all three children showed a beginning acceptance of separation. Their experiences compare favorably with those of Alison and Lesley, who appeared to be unconcerned about placement, had no outlet for their feelings, and acted out their anxieties by running away.

Conditions Associated with Responsive Interventions

An examination of the conditions surrounding workers' interventions may uncover reasons for the variability in their responsiveness to children's feelings. Conditions associated with responsiveness included reason for placement, expression of need by the child, the worker's self-awareness, and the worker's newness to child placement work.

recognized theory or principles about separation and placement. These conditions included workers becoming frustrated with parents or adolescents, having to move children for bureaucratic reasons, and experiencing uncertainty about handling separation.

Frustration with Parents or Adolescents. Ron's worker was clearly upset on Ron's behalf about his mother, who appeared to have deserted him. The worker conveyed to Ron a negative view of his mother, trying to force him to face reality. This did not seem to meet Ron's needs, as he continued to believe his mother would come back to him. If the worker had taken a gentler approach, Ron might have been able to share his sadness and confusion with the worker, who could then have provided support.

Workers may become frustrated when the reasons for placement are not socially acceptable, that is, when they reflect negatively on parents. Perhaps explicit training is needed in talking with children about upsetting topics, such as a parent's mental illness or unexplained disappearance. It is important to be realistic with children, without denigrating their parents. From the findings of this study and the literature review, we can expect that children who feel abandoned are likely to sustain hopes of being rescued by their parents. They might respond to an exploration of their feelings about their parents' absence, but would reject any direct attack on their defenses or any implied criticism of their parents.

Mike's worker showed frustration about his inability to reach Mike's feelings, referring to young people like Mike as being "just so tight and perfect that they won't get into it at all"; he also expressed a sense of powerlessness, talking in terms of "these kids" not expressing their feelings if they were hit "with a sledgehammer." There was no indication that he tried to use social work interviewing skills, which might have drawn out Mike's feelings.

The workers for Alison and Lesley expressed frustration that the girls had agreed to cooperate in foster care, then ran away.

Despite prodding from their supervisors, these workers seemed unable to look beyond the girls' behavior to consider their underlying feelings.

Bureaucratically Initiated Placement Changes. John and Jennifer's worker had to move them from a temporary to a regular home; at the same time, the worker was leaving the agency and transferring the children to another worker. Yet she asserted— and her supervisor agreed—that the children would be less disturbed than their foster carers by the move. This idea is totally contrary to accepted separation theory and suggests that the worker and supervisor may have some reason for denying reality. If they analyzed the situation, they might have to admit that the move (especially concurrent with a change of workers) would be disruptive to John and Jennifer, and that it was caused by the agency's policy of using temporary homes as first placements. If a temporary placement is expected to create separation problems for foster carers, it is hard to justify its routine use with children. The denial by the worker and supervisor that a move is potentially damaging suggests they are reluctant to consider the pain they may be causing to children.

Uncertainty about Handling Separation. The workers for both Mark and Ron expressed uncertainty about responding to separation feelings. They were aware that the boys needed help, but seemed to have little idea how to approach them. This may be a fairly widespread condition among placement workers, as the supervisors to whom they expressed their concern offered no guidance or support.

Overburdened Workers. Although no workers said they were too overburdened to help children with their feelings, a supervisor introduced this theme in a follow-up session to the training. He noted that workers admitting children to care had to expend much time and energy on instrumental tasks such as finding a placement and preparing material for court. As a result of the separation training, his team of workers decided to handle tainty, frustration, and personal reactions to separation. When they are uncertain about how to approach children, they need encouragement to use interviewing skills such as questioning, normalizing, and modeling. When they experience frustration about conditions surrounding the separation, they need help to understand their frustration so that it does not make them ineffective. Finally, workers need help to examine their personal feelings about separation: with self-knowledge, they should be better able to translate their own experiences into sensitive responses to children.

Judging from the beneficial results of providing background information to children, such openness should be part of agency protocol. Troy's worker, for example, believed the agency would not let a 15-year-old boy in long-term care see his own case record. Legislation on access to information has now affirmed the right of clients to see information the agency keeps about them. Children and youths, however, may not insist on their rights: like others in residential care, they are relatively power-less compared to workers and foster carers. The case record is a good source of information because of its detail and relative objectivity: when workers attempt to give children and youths verbal information about their past lives, they may provide an edited version that omits any information the worker considers to be potentially upsetting.

Workers who bring children into care should obtain photos and letters from the child's family, if not immediately, then soon after placement. Although many placements turn out to be short term, children who remain in care are dependent upon their first worker to preserve something of their past. The dearth of family information is illustrated in the lifebooks some agencies create for children in long-term care; those seen by the author tend to have mementoes of placements but almost nothing about the child's family. It is the agency's responsibility to ensure that information is available to children to help them integrate their past, present, and future.

Chapter Five
Agency Influence on
Children's Separation Experiences

This chapter broadens the analysis of the practices recorded in the taped sessions to include supervisory help to workers, as well as agency structures and norms that influence how separation is handled with children. The assumption in Chapter Four that workers would report all their relevant interventions was extended to this analysis of supervisors' interventions. When the tape reflected little or no response by the supervisor to a separation issue raised by the worker, it was assumed the supervisor had not responded.

Supervisory Help to Workers

Supervisors help workers to deal with their task of separating children from their families by supporting and teaching workers, and ensuring their adherence to agency norms and standards. Support is especially important to workers in handling the pressure they often experience from all parties to a foster care placement. The supervisor may have to be proactive, rather than simply reactive to the workers' requests for help. Reactive support depends on workers' identification of separation issues and their willingness to discuss them in supervision. As shown in Chapter Four, some workers may minimize the importance of separation to children or fail to elicit children's feelings. Proactive supervisors will provide leadership in ways that do not threaten workers, but strengthen their resolve and capacity to deal with separation issues.

In their teaching role, supervisors help workers to integrate separation theory and research findings with their practice by reminding workers to use the knowledge and skills they have already acquired. They provide information to fill gaps in workers' knowledge of theory and practice and influence attitudes by modeling a responsive approach to children with separation problems. The supervisors' effectiveness in these tasks depends upon their own understanding of the field and their level of comfort with handling the pain involved in separating children from their families.

Supervisors also monitor the quality of workers' practice. They convey agency norms, especially to new workers, and evaluate workers' practice to ensure that it meets basic standards. Supervisors are usually the final arbiters of placement decisions; they have decision-making power about the admission of children to care and subsequent re-placements, as well as family contact and reunion. The case excerpts below illustrate supervisory interventions with workers concerning separation.

Supporting Workers in Facilitating Child-Family Communication

Workers may need encouragement to work at maintaining contact between children and their families. Parents often need help with transportation to visit their children; this task can consume a great deal of the worker's limited time and energy.

> Maria and Rocco's mother had just entered a psychiatric facility, and could not initially visit them in foster care. The supervisor suggested that the worker make an extra effort to maintain the contact by visiting the hospital himself: "Will you be able to see the mother and bring word from her if she can't come herself?" The worker said he would.

Encouraging the worker to make extra trips to maintain links between children and their parents is important; such work is not easily undertaken in the climate of strained resources that is characteristic of child welfare agencies.

Urging Workers to Confront Children

In Ron's case, the worker seemed to be insensitive in pointing out to Ron that his mother had shown little interest in him and comparing this to the care given by the agency. Yet the supervisor suggested that the worker be even more confrontational with Ron than he had been.

> Ron, eight, had last seen his mother four months earlier, when she apparently abandoned him. The worker said she "had a pattern of dropping out for months and then reappearing." Ron continued to anticipate his mother's return and was finding it difficult to get on with his life. The supervisor's advice, as mentioned earlier was, "You see at some point you're going to have to say, 'Look kid, your mother's not coming back.'" She explained further, "I would expect this kid to have a heck of a lot of anger in him. At some point, for him to ever succeed anywhere, he's going to need an opportunity to vent this kind of anger."
>
> The supervisor repeated her advice: "I guess at some point you have to say, 'I think that Mother's doing more than just looking at other affairs. She's left you, kid.' He's got to come to grips with that." Later she explained, "He's just got to talk about it. This is the kind of kid who could go through life without forming any really meaningful relationships because he'd be too afraid…I don't think we should allow this to happen with this kid." The worker was uncertain about the confrontation, saying, "The only thing that keeps me from doing this is that I'm afraid it would be more damaging, because he's very rigid about the fact that his mother hasn't left him."

The supervisor's assessment that Ron needed to face reality about his mother before he could move on to other relationships is sound. Her suggested intervention, however, ignores the principle of starting where the client is. As Ron is still hoping for his mother's return, her confrontational approach would probably be very threatening and cause him to strengthen his defenses. The supervisor may have been underestimating Ron's sense of loss, in assuming that he was ready for confrontation; she may also have been angry with his mother for disappearing, judging from her blunt approach and her pessimism. This interpretation implies that supervisors of foster care practice, as well as workers, should examine their personal feelings about separation and parents' behavior toward their children.

Teaching Workers to Elicit Children's Feelings

In the following case, the worker described for his supervisor his unsuccessful attempts to encourage a youth to express feelings about separation.

> Wayne, 14, was placed in care by his father and stepmother; he tried to contact his mother who lived with his siblings but could not find her. Wayne's behavior showed he was upset, but he denied this when the worker asked direct questions about his feelings, for example, "Do you feel angry?" As the worker said, "He just brings down the iron curtain."
>
> The supervisor suggested ways of helping Wayne deal with his feelings: "You can try generalizing by saying, 'You know I've seen other boys in your position and they were very disappointed like this when they weren't able to visit'; or you could model for him, 'If I were in your position I would feel very sad or angry...that I didn't know where my mother was or my sister or brother...I'd be pretty angry or sad or both.'"

It was helpful that Wayne's worker had tried to reach his feelings, and was willing to ask for help with this. The supervisor assumed a teaching role, citing the techniques of generalizing or modeling, and giving examples to help the worker act on these suggestions.

In another case, the worker expressed uncertainty about how to approach children about their mother being in jail.

> Melinda, seven, and her brother Randy, five, were placed in care when their mother went to jail. They communicated very little with their foster carers, and the worker was not sure what to say to them about their mother. The supervisor suggested, "Did you ever use reassurance or try to clarify the situation to the kids or just mention their feelings without pushing them too much? For example, you might use the old standard, 'Sounds like you are upset about that?'" The worker added, "Maybe I could project or label the kids' feelings for them."

This supervisor suggested two traditional interviewing techniques: clarification and reflection of clients' feelings. As with the first supervisor, she was describing basic interviewing skills with which a trained worker should be familiar; in fact, the worker for Melinda and Randy was able to conceptualize additional practice possibilities. Yet both workers needed help to approach the children's feelings. This supports Steinhauer's [1974] hypothesis that workers may lose their ability to intervene effectively when confronted by children who are experiencing the loss of their parents.

The supervisor in the case of Melinda and Randy could have been more specific about clarifying the situation. The worker was understandably hesitant to talk with the children about their mother being in jail; yet child welfare workers are often in situations where society has brought sanctions against parents, causing children to be admitted to care. If this topic is avoided, the children may assume that the reason they are in care is too terrible to be discussed. Furthermore, in the absence of an explanation, they will be inclined to blame themselves for the breakup of their family.

Reinforcing Workers' Knowledge

Another supervisor simply supported the worker's own understanding of a child's separation reactions.

> Kevin, nine, had an eating disorder that seemed worse when he returned to the foster home after each visit with his mother, and the foster carer was pressing to have visiting reduced. The supervisor interpreted Kevin's behavior as a reaction to separation: "He is separated from his mother, he's getting along well with his foster mother, but he is probably going through feelings of being separated from his mother." The worker agreed, "Oh, I think he does…everytime he has a visit and he has to go back, there is the separation again." The supervisor suggested further that the eating disorder was probably "the evidence of his anxiety or sadness."

Although no conclusion was reached in this session about handling the foster carer's objections, the supervisor's formulation did not support the foster carer's proposal to reduce visits. The worker's readiness to agree suggests that she had made the same assessment, but needed reinforcement to deal with the foster carer's objections.

Ensuring that Recognized Practice Is Followed: Providing Children with Background Information

Supervisors generally have more experience with agency practices and with recognized standards of casework and can be expected to note what workers may overlook.

> Corey, 14, questioned his worker about his past, and she told him that he came into care because "his mother was a

16-year-old who couldn't care for him...right now I'm having a terrible time with him, and he's trying to find his mother." The supervisor did not give specific direction, but implied that the worker should help Corey fill in the pieces of his past. She said, "Corey is mixed up, feeling so confused and at such a loss that he is really saying, 'Who am I?' It's hard to know who you are and where you're headed if you don't know where you're coming from."

Most workers and supervisors would recognize that children need information about their origins, but this supervisor was exceptional in making the link with Corey's orientation to the future. Her view is supported by the comment of a man in his thirties who, at a child welfare conference attended by the author, discussed his search for parents. He said the gap in his past had made him feel like "a spot in time," and he had found it difficult to make plans for the future, until he located his family a year earlier.

Helping Workers to Counter Foster Carers' Exclusion of Families

Workers sometimes have to deal with foster carers' attitudes that interfere with the agency's plans for a child.

Andrea, eight, was about to return to her mother, who was being discharged from a psychiatric hospital; in the past the agency had been satisfied with the care provided by the mother, although she was periodically hospitalized for depression. As the worker explained, Andrea's foster carer was openly negative about the reunion, and Andrea was beginning to show doubts about whether her mother could care for her. The supervisor suggested, "Maybe there is something you [the worker] can do to stop her discouraging Andrea from the reunion."

Although the worker and supervisor had decided to return Andrea to her mother, the worker was allowing the foster carer to undermine this plan. The supervisor offered support to the worker, encouraging her to take a stand with the foster carer. The discussion, however, was somewhat inconclusive; no specific suggestions were made about how to stop the foster carer from discouraging the reunion.

Agency Practices and Service Structures

Agency placement practices are determined partly by child welfare legislation, under which placement decisions may be open to judicial scrutiny. Agencies do have a great deal of control, however, over all the parties to a placement, especially when parents request agency help directly. Agencies may set up service structures to organize their work, and develop norms and policies that guide their relationships with families and foster carers. The various aspects of structure and relationships discussed below are (1) providing continuity for children, (2) including/excluding families, (3) influencing foster carers, and (4) handling external pressures to move children.

Providing or Failing to Provide Continuity to Children in Care

When agencies take children into care, it is assumed that the agencies can offer those children a stable placement to meet their basic needs, and an ongoing relationship with a social worker. A number of children in this study experienced a series of homes and workers, and their workers commented on the cumulative effects on the children—anxiety about independence, identity confusion, and loss of contact with biological families.

Kinship Care. A few children were placed with relatives, thus reducing the degree of their separation from family. They could be expected to have fewer identity problems than children who went to live with strangers.

> Celia, 14, was placed with her maternal aunt and uncle, who had already been foster carers for another CAS. Celia was

in care, according to her worker, "as a result of a lot of extended family problems, particularly the sexual abuse of her stepbrother by Celia's mother's boyfriend. The abuse became known at a time when Celia was visiting with her aunt and uncle here in the Toronto area. She refused to go home, so eventually we apprehended [sic] her, let her stay with her aunt, and made her a Crown ward on her insistence."

"Celia agreed to see her mother a total of four times over the first four months following the court hearing. Right after the fourth visit I asked if she wanted another contact and she said, 'No.' It's probably the most ideal arrangement: she is blood-related to the woman she is living with and there are two other teenage girls in the family, who are very supportive of her. Celia's mother was actively involved in the abuse of her stepson; he had been the son of her second husband, and had been left with Celia's mother when this marriage broke up. Apparently the abused boy was the last in a series of stepsiblings and Celia was next on the list. It's very hard to say whether in fact she was abused. There's a good possibility that she was…in any case, she is really full of revulsion with respect to the mother and the stuff that went on. Secondly, I think that she is genuinely extremely frightened of her mother. The mother, according to my information and my brief contacts, can be very manipulative and very threatening in her own right."

The use of Celia's relatives as foster carers was not initiated by the agency, but exemplifies the benefits of kinship care. Celia apparently felt secure with her relatives, judging from her apparent ability to make important decisions that involved separation from her mother, first to live apart, then to cut off visits. This was the only reported case in the study where a child made it known that he or she did not want to see a parent. Possibly Celia was able to transfer her allegiance and identification to her aunt and uncle, when she felt unsafe with her mother and stepfather.

Kinship care has obvious advantages for children, as it allows for continuity in terms of family history and identity. In the U.S., its use has grown dramatically. Some agencies may be reluctant to use kinship placements because they often do not offer the same material standards as traditional foster homes; others may be biased against the relatives of parents who have had difficulty caring for their children. In the author's experience, workers are sometimes cautious about using kinship placements because of existing or potential conflicts between the parents and the related caregivers. The same exclusive attitudes that cause problems in regular foster care may be heightened when there is a history of competition or jealousy between the two parts of a family. This scenario could be avoided if parents are encouraged to search for a suitable foster home themselves: they might prefer to place their child with relatives rather than in an unknown foster home. If so, they would be likely to cooperate in making the arrangement a success.

Changing Homes and Workers. Janet and Corey were two young people in the study who had experienced an unconscionable number of changes in homes and workers.

> Janet, 18, had lived in 20 homes, and had had 16 different social workers by the time she reached the age for leaving care. During her last 18 months in care, her worker became aware of Janet's anxiety about leaving CAS care. She felt that for Janet, the agency [the building that housed the workers and administrators] was a home; even the receptionist was an important person for Janet and others like her because "she's nice to them" and "every time they come in she remembers them." This worker concluded, in discussion with an experienced colleague, that children exposed to many different homes and workers were likely to attach themselves to the agency, this being the only stable element in their lives.

Janet's anxiety about separating from the agency is understandable in terms of developmental theory. Normal adolescent growth involves seeking autonomy from parents gradually; concurrently, peer relationships become increasingly important, providing a support network for youths as they gradually assume responsibility for themselves. Janet had a series of short-term caregivers, so her only stable object of attachment was the agency, which was about to withdraw its support, suddenly and totally. Many child welfare agencies provide short-term programs to support youths as they move to independent living, and Janet might qualify for continuing financial assistance. But she would no longer have a formal connection with the workers or foster carers who could give her ongoing support and guidance. Her place with them would be filled by another young person, and Janet would be unusual if she maintained an ongoing personal connection with the agency.

> Corey, 14, had been through ten placements and 20 social workers in his years with the agency. The supervisor noted that Corey did not know where he had been or how many placement breakdowns he had experienced. He couldn't remember "who did what," which left him with "the big question, 'Who am I?'"

Normally, teenagers who have moved frequently with their families can be expected to have memories of their various houses and neighborhoods. Corey's inability to remember how many homes he had experienced suggests that he may be protecting himself against the feelings associated with so many changes. He may have repressed painful memories, such as being rejected by caregivers; he may also have learned to protect himself by not engaging with the families with whom he lived. Corey's case illustrates that workers cannot assume that children in care have knowledge of even their recent past. It also adds strength to earlier arguments for ensuring that children in care know their own histories. Corey's identity confusion is understandable in view of the disruptions in his environment. The comfort of adolescents with increasing independence depends partly on their ability to form a stable autonomous identity.

Failing to Protect Child-Family Links. Another aspect of worker change is that children may view the worker who first places them as representing their only ties with their family. Moreover, because of an agency's structural specialization, the children may lose this person at the same time that they lose a familiar home.

> Chris, 12, was being moved to an institution because his behavior had become increasingly unmanageable in the foster home. His worker, who was also responsible for dealing with Chris's family, noted that she would not be having further contact with Chris, because another worker was responsible for the agency's liaison with this particular institution.

In effect, Chris was exposed to two crucial changes at once. Not only did he have to adjust to an unfamiliar and totally different environment, but he lost a familiar worker. It is also significant that this worker was the link with his family.

The foregoing cases recall the earlier discussion about bureaucratically caused changes of placements and workers. Not all the changes experienced by Janet and Corey would have been caused by bureaucratic structures; staff turnover also causes many worker changes. In good economic times, many urban Ontario Children's Aid Societies have a worker turnover rate of 30% to 40% a year, probably because of the relatively low pay and high stress in the child welfare field.

Agencies deciding to admit children into care tend to compare the children's experiences in chaotic, neglectful, or abusive families with the stability the agencies assume they can provide—a caring worker and a lasting placement. When this projected stability turns out to be a series of changing workers and homes, the benefits of placement rapidly diminish. Decisions about child placement should be viewed in this context. As well, the changeability in the foster care system emphasizes how crucial it is to keep children in touch with their families, both physically and psychologically.

Including/Excluding Families

The attitudes of agencies and foster carers to children's ongoing family relationships were wide-ranging: some welcomed family involvement in children's lives, others clearly wanted to exclude them.

Allowing Contact to Lapse. The legislation covering foster care in Ontario supports family visiting. It is based on the principle of "least intrusive" intervention into families and cultural continuity for children. Further, judges are directed to make a ruling on parental access when they award custody of a child to a CAS. Yet a number of cases described by workers seemed to have a default option of "no visiting," that is, a clear case had to be made in favor of contact before workers took any initiative.

Sometimes the agency seemed to make no arrangements for visits until the child insisted.

> Jason, 12, seemed to have to struggle to be allowed to see his family. According to the worker, "He was very abrupt, very demanding, very persistent, very questioning, asking, 'When am I going to see my parents?' He phoned me up and put me on the spot." Jason even threatened his worker with lawyers if visits were not arranged. These requests were eventually met, and the worker commented that Jason's level of trust had increased greatly because "he knows he's going to have the visits. He knows that they are on a regular basis. He knows when they are going to be arranged. He knows the only reason a visit will be canceled will be the parents pulling out." Jason's worker noted also that his increased trust was "extending to the world...he's also more trusting of the school...the foster parents."

In view of the worker's comments about the positive effects of visiting on Jason, it is significant that she offered no reason why visits were initially withheld. Although Jason's assertiveness made this case unusual, the worker's implicit consideration of "no visiting" as a default option accords with the author's experience with CASs in the course of this research. In verbal discussion and case records, workers frequently recommended that family contacts should be planned "as appropriate"; when requested to explain this, workers tended to define "appropriate" in terms of parents behaving well and children not being upset by contact with them.

Some parents appeared to have deserted their children, and there was no evidence that workers reached out to find these parents. In one case, the agency response to a parent's reappearance seemed to be negative.

> Eric, 15, had immigrated from Newfoundland to Ontario with his parents, who requested his placement in foster care when he became difficult for them to handle. Subsequently, Eric's father lost his job and the family returned to Newfoundland without Eric, making no plans with the CAS for his return. A few months later, the father reappeared. As described by Eric's worker, "The family worker told me that the father 'popped' into the office...apparently from Newfoundland. Apparently he was very jovial with the family worker, saying, 'Hi! How are you!' as though he had never been gone. Anyway, he wants to see Eric; but the family worker wasn't sure if we should pursue this, as he felt the father had just dumped Eric. We discussed this but it was left with nothing being done."

> "I talked to Eric about this development, telling him, 'The negative news is that we have heard from your father.' He sounded very matter-of-fact, saying, 'Oh...is he here?' and I affirmed that he is back in Toronto, that 'he came to see John [the family worker], talked to him, and asked about you. He was very anxious to see you. I don't know how you feel.' He said 'Okay' without a lot of emotion, so I asked 'Are you saying you'd like to see your dad?' He said, 'Yes.' I said 'Okay, I will tell the family worker that you would like to see

your dad and you would like to see your brother, whom I know you want to see.'"

This excerpt reveals the worker's ambivalence about Eric's family. He seemed enthusiastic about a sibling visit, yet joined with another worker in expressing negativity toward Eric seeing his father, defining the father's appearance as "negative news." The family worker sounded punitive toward the father, apparently suggesting no visit be granted because the father had "dumped" Eric. The workers' negativism seems to be linked to the father's treatment of Eric—leaving Eric behind, suddenly and without explanation. Although the worker sought Eric's opinion, there was little indication that either worker validated his right— or possible need—to see his father. The supervisor made no response, suggesting that this case did not diverge from normal agency policy.

As noted earlier in the literature review, parents may be discouraged from visiting if they are limited to the agency premises.

Mrs. M. was the mother of two children in care. Her worker "suggested that the initial visits be at the agency. Mrs. M. was not really in favor of that, but did not want to visit in the foster home. At that point I didn't feel up to taking the children to where she was living. So we had two appointments set up and the mother broke them both."

The mother's unreliability in keeping the appointments could be interpreted as disinterest in her children or it could be an aversion to the restrictions placed on her visits. It seems more likely to be the latter, as her interest in the children was shown by her initiative in maintaining communication with them.

As the worker said, "We did establish that Mrs. M. would phone on a Monday evening between seven-thirty and eight o'clock...just to talk to the children...and she has done this. The foster mother reports that they're very calm after their mother talks to them." The supervisor noted, "The kids have not had any word from Mom as to why they had to leave home. You really haven't had the opportunity to get them together." The worker responded, "No, and I don't know what she is talking about when she talks to them over the phone."

The supervisor implied that it was important to have Mrs. M. explain the separation to her children, but allowed the subject to lapse at this point. As a representative of the agency viewpoint, the supervisor also seems to have condoned the worker's approach in allowing the case to drift to no visiting. A supervisor who was committed to established practice principles would presumably have encouraged maintenance of contact, as well as discussion between mother and children about the separation and reasons for it. The lack of supervisory intervention may reflect a lack of agency commitment to accepted theories of separation and placement principles. There may also be an element of work overload that hindered better handling of visits, as the worker commented, "I didn't feel up to..." When a CAS worker is confronted with too many case demands, it is likely that parental visits with placed children will be given low priority, because parents and children have little power in the organization.

Ignoring Ambiguous or Negative Foster Carer Attitudes. Children's family ties will be facilitated or discouraged by the attitudes of foster carers; the latter are open to influence from their agencies. Some workers tried to encourage positive attitudes.

Vince, 15, had foster carers who, according to his worker, were "not accepting of his parents...I think that they are very angry and they're resentful that the parents could have done something like this [not explained] to Vince." With the worker's help, the foster carers were able to be "accepting of the whole of Vince's situation, including his family.

> The message that Vince gets is, 'We care for you and so we want you to have these visits. We can't say anything about your parents because we don't know them.'"

Vince's worker was proactive in communicating to his foster carers that his family was important to him, and she reported success in getting them to accept that Vince's family was part of his whole "situation." It is interesting to view this from Vince's standpoint. Would it seem to him that his foster carers' assertion of their "neutrality" was a denial of their true feelings, or perhaps a sign of disinterest in him? People who are close to us usually try to convey a positive attitude toward our parents, even those unknown to them, in deference to their interest in us.

A "neutral" attitude toward parents also creates an obstacle when children want to discuss their family relationships with foster carers.

> Kim, 16, attempted to talk with her foster carers about her relationship with her parents. Since she talked more openly to her foster carers than to her worker, the supervisor suggested that the worker might provide guidance to them: "Have you discussed with the foster parents any particular direction they might take in discussing Kim's feelings when she brings them up?" The worker had not: "No, I haven't pressured or guided them in taking a side or discussing this with Kim. I've kind of condoned their feeling of wanting 'to listen' only and not get involved, because they feel, unless they really know the parents, that's not their role." The supervisor made no further suggestions about how Kim might be helped.

The supervisor showed initiative at first in encouraging the worker to guide the foster carers in helping Kim. When the worker seemed at a loss for direction, however, the supervisor allowed the subject to lapse. In effect, the agency seemed to accept the foster carers' approach of not becoming involved in discussing Kim's feelings about her parents. This left Kim without much support in her efforts to resolve feelings about her family.

Some workers did not challenge foster carers' negative attitudes toward parents, although these would probably create conflicting loyalties for children.

> Todd, seven, was in care because he had been abused and neglected by a substitute caregiver in his home. Although there was no evidence of abuse by his mother, the worker observed that "Todd's foster mother has an evil picture of his mother." The worker was puzzled about the source of this negative picture, "because I've not painted one." He concluded that the foster carer was influenced by "her protective feeling toward Todd."

It is natural for foster carers to be protective of children living in their homes, and to have negative feelings toward those who may have neglected or abused the children. The attitude of Todd's foster carer sounds extreme, however, and there is no apparent basis for it. If the social worker's account is accurate, it seems that the "evil picture" may have been created by the foster carer herself: possibly this was her defense against the threat that Todd's mother might try to reclaim him. The social worker's apparent lack of intervention to influence the foster carer's attitude is cause for concern: Todd could hardly benefit from having his caregiver define his mother as "evil."

In another case, a foster carer made her negative feelings explicitly known to the children, and agency intervention was ineffective in controlling this.

> Samantha, 11, and Ashley, nine, were sisters placed in the same home. Their worker reported, "The foster mother got across to the children her own fear of their parents and reinforced some of what they were feeling. She also made remarks that put the parents down in front of the children." The supervisor asked, "Did you try to stop that?" The worker had tried unsuccessfully: "Yes, on two occasions I

attempted to discuss it with her; she was certainly open to discussing it, but I don't think that this really changed anything between herself and the children."

This worker was clearly concerned that the foster carer's comments would have ill effects on Samantha and Ashley's relationship with their parents. As she said, "I think the foster parents' attitude toward the parents affected the children very much. I think some of this is normal, but I have felt over the last six months that if there were any chance of reuniting these children with their parents we would have to move them from that home."

Despite the worker's persistent feeling that the foster carers' negative attitude was an obstacle to the family's reunion, she seemed ineffectual in the situation. She appeared to feel hopeless about changing the foster carers' attitudes, or at least unwilling to confront them. Instead, she proposed to solve the problem by moving the girls, which seems to be a desperate measure in terms of separation theory.

There are indications that the case described above is not unusual: first, the worker described the foster carer's feelings as somewhat "normal"; second, the supervisor made no comment about the worker's perception that the only solution would be to move the children. This suggests that the situation was within agency norms, and the foster carer would be allowed to continue influencing the girls against their family.

Protecting Foster Carers. The agencies in the study tried to protect foster carers by restricting parent-child communication, as well as by supporting the caregivers' status as substitute parents. Parents were sometimes directed not to try to contact their children in foster care. A mother of children in care (outside the study) revealed to the author her perception that the agency would allow her to send them presents at Christmas, but would not tell her children the presents were from her. An example from the study follows.

Danny, 14, entered foster care because his mother, a single parent, could not handle him. Her inability to make him comply with his diet for diabetes was a particular problem. The worker said, "At first I thought this would be a good situation where Danny's mother could visit him in the foster home, but now I realize she is not a suitable parent to do this…she would be phoning at all times of the night asking, 'What is Danny eating?' and being just too concerned over what was going on. It would be a mistake to have her in touch with the foster mother…I even question now whether the two of them should meet."

The supervisor did not accept the worker's categorical rejection of contact. Instead, she suggested, "If it's going to work, then you would have to spend a lot of time with both the mother and the foster mother, maybe dealing with their feelings about each other." This seemed to influence the worker, who then noted that Danny's foster carer accepted paternal visits with another child in her home. The supervisor was not sure this implied acceptance for Danny's mother; she suggested that maybe "in that case the foster mother felt sorry for the father because it's more difficult to expect a man to parent," and the worker agreed.

The supervisor also introduced the question of Danny's future: "Does Danny plan to go home to his mother?" and the worker thought he eventually would do so. I think the big struggle between the two of them is Danny's diet…one of the problems is Danny going home for a weekend visit and the mother compensating by letting him have too much sugar. Then he's got problems with the sugar in his urine after the weekend visit. After the last weekend visit, Danny brought cookies back with him that his mother made. Part of the problem is that his mother has less money to buy the type of food Danny needs, while the foster mother is probably giving him foods that are better for him." As the supervisor commented, "So you've got a tug-of-war about who is going to be right and who is going to take the best care of Danny."

The main problem here is whether the mother should be excluded, not just from the foster home, but from even meeting her son's foster carer. The worker seemed to think she had to protect the foster carer from having to deal with Danny's mother. The agency appeared to expect ideal behavior from parents as a precondition for visiting their children in a foster home. Yet it would be confusing for Danny to have to deal with two caregivers who did not even know each other.

Another point of interest is the reported discrepancy between the foster carer's attitude toward Danny's mother and her sympathy toward a visiting father. The supervisor and worker both expected the foster carer to be judgmental toward Danny's mother for failing to give adequate care, while excusing the father of another child on grounds of his gender. This reflects an acceptance of sexist attitudes in society generally.

Finally, the economic base for providing Danny with an appropriate diet was apparently available to his foster carer, but not to his mother. This suggests that our society stops short of supporting children with health problems at a level that might allow them to stay in their own homes, while providing this support in out-of-home care.

Some workers demonstrated protectiveness of foster carers' status as substitute parents, as shown by their acceptance of children using parental titles.

> Angel, six, called both her foster carer and mother "Mom." According to the worker, the foster carer was reluctant to cooperate with home visits, and Angel "was confused because of the moving back and forth...all the visits home, and calling foster mom Mom while calling her mother Mom. Everytime I went to pick her up in the car it was, 'Where are we going, where are we going?' She'd say that

about 12 times in the car, then I would have to repeat, 'We're going to see Mom.' The only way I could identify her real mother was to include the dog...'Mom and Mimi.' Then it seemed that for Angel it would click in which mom it was."

Angel's repeated questioning of the worker suggests that she is anxious about her situation. The expectation or acceptance by others that Angel call the foster carer Mom may have signified to her that her mother had been permanently replaced. Even at six, she would probably assume that children have only one mother. In view of Angel's apparent anxiety, it is noteworthy that neither the worker nor supervisor questioned the continuing use of this confusing terminology. Agencies may encourage or condone the use of parental titles because it gives status to foster carers. In effect, it implies that the child belongs to them, thus providing some compensation for the work of foster care in the absence of adequate pay.

Children's parents are likely to feel defensive in their dealings with foster carers if they feel their role is being usurped. Agencies seem to find it natural to support foster carers, but may be insensitive to the feelings of parents. The following incident involved Danny.

The worker said, "Danny telephoned his mother from the foster home and talked for a long time; when she eventually said she couldn't talk any longer, Danny paid no attention. Then the foster mother approached the phone saying, 'Hang up now, son,' and Danny immediately responded, 'Gotta go, Mom.'" On hearing this, the supervisor laughed [presumably about the confusing "mother-son" terminology], saying, "That's beautiful!" The worker laughed too, but added "the mother was furious at hearing the foster mother call Danny 'son.'" The worker observed, "Danny knows he has to listen to the foster mother and doesn't

face early in the placement. That didn't occur to me, but I've thought about it since. Whether that would have changed things—it well might have—it certainly made a big difference with Rick's placement when I used that approach."

From this worker's report, and the supervisor's lack of response, it seems to be normal agency practice to tell foster carers the negative aspects of children's family experiences. Although it is important to pass on information about children's background, their parents' serious failings should be placed in context; otherwise, caregivers may make negative judgments about the family. Ideally, background information should be given in the presence of children's families, or it should be framed in the context of environmental problems such as poverty and gaps in the parents' own socialization experiences.

When he placed Rick, the worker tried to convey a more favorable view of the family to the foster carers and was successful. It is unclear whether he took Rick's parents to the foster home, but this is one means of letting foster carers see that the child's parents are human beings. In this way, negative stereotyping, which can be damaging to the child's family, can be minimized.

Countering Foster Carers' Resistance. Although a number of workers and supervisors expressed theoretical acceptance of inclusive fostering, very few seemed to be implementing this in practice. They had to be willing to deal with foster carers' resistance to family involvement.

> One worker stated, "I think it's really important that a worker let the foster parents know that visiting is important, whether they're ready for it or not. We should start dealing with that, for sure, because some [foster carers] say, 'That's never happened before' and 'I hope they [parents] don't go off the deep end, because I won't like it' or 'I can't handle it.'"

Another worker went beyond willingness into action by

affirming a father's right to be involved: "It was such a hassle...the foster mother didn't agree with father visiting in their home...yet she didn't approve of him taking the children out of the home, because she thought they weren't ready for that...it was a difficult struggle." The supervisor reinforced this worker's account with praise: "But you worked that through...you straightened that out...it was good service to the kids...giving them some security, reassuring them, trying to label their feelings and bringing Dad back into the picture."

These two workers experienced tension between their adherence to practice principles and the resistance of foster carers, who clung to an accustomed exclusiveness. These workers did incorporate their principles with their practice, however, and their supervisors reinforced their efforts.

Modeling the Inclusion of Parents. A solution to foster carer resistance was found by a worker who brought the carers and parents together as part of the child's preplacement visit to the foster home.

Trevor, six, was brought to a new foster home by his worker and father. The worker noted, "When you have the Dad in the room...you get so much concrete and firsthand information transferred from Dad to the foster parents. So the cards are on the table and they know exactly what's going on. While we were there I almost took a back seat...if there was something that wasn't clear, if Dad had said something in a kind of a backward way, then I would want to clarify it for myself and the foster parents; sometimes the foster parents explained it to me. Once the ball got rolling [the two sets of parents] were able to communicate. The foster parents had all kinds of questions to ask and there was really no need for me to get too involved."

The supervisor supported this approach: "It's a lot

easier…and I'm sure Dad would feel a lot better. Also the foster parents would feel a lot better." No mention was made of Trevor, but he seemed to feel good too, as he voluntarily hugged the female foster carer during the visit.

The foregoing suggests that inclusiveness was not usual practice for this agency: the worker's detailed account, and the supervisor's use of the comparative words "easier" and "better" indicate that it was not the norm to bring parents on a preplacement visit.

The rarity of parent accompaniment was also illustrated by the worker's and supervisor's reactions to its apparent success.

The worker said, "Things were going too well. Like there's something just not 'kosher' here." The supervisor agreed, "That was my feeling when you started too, like you always become leery when kids start to do things like that [hugging the new foster carer on a first visit]."

It would probably be reassuring to Trevor to see his father and the foster carer talking cooperatively about arrangements for his care. This basis for an ongoing relationship between his caregivers would free him of the loyalty conflicts experienced by many children in care.

As the worker reported: "Anyway, that's what happened and at the end the foster father said to the father, 'We want you to become a member of our extended family, you know, because that's the way that we feel it has to be in order to make sure that Trevor goes back home successfully.' The foster parents really are going over halfway, I don't know how many foster parents would do this."

The worker's inclusion of Trevor's father in the preplacement visit led to cooperation between the two sets of caregivers. Trevor's foster carers were unusual in suggesting that his father become part of their extended family. This could, however, be a common outcome of an inclusive approach to placement, if foster carers view themselves as paraprofessionals and accept the goal of children being reunited with their families.

Not all parents would be as cooperative Trevor's father with their child's foster carers. As the literature review has shown, it can be very painful for parents to see someone else caring for their children and they may back away. From the child's viewpoint, however, the presence of their parents in an unfamiliar place would be reassuring. Moreover, parental accompaniment demonstrates to children that their parents accept the inevitability, if not the desirability, of the placement. If their parents do not come to the home, children may feel they have been "kidnapped" by the agency. This can lead them to hope persistently that their parents will eventually rescue them, as shown earlier in the case of Ron, whose mother had disappeared.

It should be mentioned here that Trevor's worker and the worker for Maria and Rocco were the only two in the study who explicitly associated their interventions with ideas they had gained in the project training. Interestingly, they were two of the newest workers in the study. It may be that they received the training before being conditioned to exclusive practice by long-standing agency norms. This has implications for providing training at an early point, at the same time as influencing agencywide practice by a broad-based approach that includes placement resource workers and foster carers in the training.

Handling External Pressure to Move Children

Agencies occasionally have to move children quickly for reasons of safety, and they are forced to violate placement principles. In the cases below, no safety matters were mentioned, yet agencies responded to pressure from foster carers or parents as though they were powerless to make child-centered decisions. Specifically, they acquiesced to parental requests to admit difficult adolescents to care, and to caregivers' demands for immediate removal of a child.

Rushing Placement under Pressure. Agencies may be pressured from outside to treat the placement of a child as an emergency. In capitulating to such pressures, they may violate their own placement principles.

> Benny, 12, lived with his single-parent mother who felt his behavior was out of her control. He was to appear in juvenile court for a minor first offense. As the worker said, "Benny was telling me he couldn't stand living at home any longer, and his mother was saying she could not control him any longer. The mother wanted Benny admitted, on an emergency basis, as soon as there was a vacancy."

> In response to the supervisor's queries, the worker acknowledged, "I didn't feel it was really an emergency...I thought there should be some planning involved. The conditions at home were pretty negative, but I felt they could have held out until a suitable home was found. We wanted to include the planning aspect of Benny's admission to care... but the parents pressed, so I picked him up at court, after his court hearing, and brought him directly to an emergency placement."

There seems to have been no child-centered reason to treat Benny's placement as an emergency. The worker could have taken time to find a long-term suitable home and to arrange a preplacement visit for Benny and his mother. Although Benny was pushing for placement, it is likely that he would prefer a permanent placement rather than face the prospect of having to move a second time. He would also benefit from a preplacement visit, which would help him to absorb the effects of the move gradually. With respect to Benny's parents, they may have pressed for immediate placement so they could offer this alternative to the court in order to avoid a stiff sentence for Benny. Again, this does not seem to be sufficient reason to contravene accepted practice. The worker clearly had misgivings, but she acquiesced to the multiple pressures. As workers rarely make placement decisions alone, the agency must also have yielded to the external pressure to treat the placement as an emergency.

Meeting the Needs of Parents or Caregivers. Some placement decisions, especially those involving adolescents, were motivated more by the wishes of parents than the needs of children. The agency might resist at first, but eventually acceded to the parents' demands.

> Tara, 13, had become a problem after her mother's remarriage the previous year. She habitually ran away and been truant from school. The worker attributed her behavior to "difficulty adjusting to a new stepparent, and to a teenaged stepbrother, whom she thought was being favored over herself. For 12 years of her life she was alone with her mother…this was a big change. The way it looked to Tara [and actually to her mother, too] was that her stepfather was calling the shots along with his son. The stepfather was telling Tara what to do and putting her down a great deal, and Tara's mother was not allowed to interfere."

> After hearing this, the supervisor suggested that the family's plight might have been handled by a referral to family counseling. Then the worker pressured the supervisor, saying there was "a tremendous need for Tara to be removed from the family" and that Tara and her mother also "thought that way." The supervisor apparently capitulated, as Tara was admitted to care.

Although Tara apparently agreed to be placed, the situation seems to have been out of her control. Her mother may have been trying to protect her from the verbal abuse of her stepfather, who seemed to have all the power in the home. The mother may have viewed Tara's removal as a way to reduce stress in the family, because she did not seem able to assert herself with her new husband. The supervisor's suggestion of family counseling was sound, as the request for placement seems to have arisen from the stepfather's reactions to Tara. But the worker passed on the pressure she was experiencing from the family, and the supervisor capitulated. In effect, the agency eventually joined the mother in acceding to the wishes of the stepfather.

In the next case, a stepfather was forcing the mother to make a choice between him and her daughter.

> Laurie, 10, was living with her mother in a second marriage, and was viewed by her mother as undermining this union. As reported by the worker, "Mother was saying, 'I can't handle it...my husband said either Laurie goes or he's going to leave.'" The worker appraised the situation as follows: "Laurie is so dependent on her mother that she doesn't give the parents any free time at all. She doesn't go out and play with other kids, she's always at home with the parents, so the parents don't have any time for their own lives. They're feeling that if Laurie were out of the house it would be better for her as well as for them. Mother is afraid of being left alone eventually...she said, 'In five or six years Laurie is going to be gone. She's going to be 16 years old and I'm going to be left with nobody. My husband's going to leave me if I keep her.'"

> The worker continued, "At that time, considering I didn't know what was going to happen that night and both parents were drinking, I thought maybe it would be better if we took her into care...I really think Laurie herself would have been all right staying at home, but with the parents there may have been an explosion. It wasn't that I thought something was going to happen to Laurie, but just that I thought the parents needed the time to discuss what was going on, because Laurie was one of the major problems over which they were in disagreement. Also, Laurie is always there to listen to their disagreement and arguing. I think she should go into care."

Laurie, like Tara, would be moved into a strange home, apparently because she had become a focus of conflict in a second marriage. Unlike Tara, Laurie gave no sign of wanting to move; in fact, her extreme dependency on her mother suggests that separation would be traumatic for her. Again, the agency might have insisted that the parents seek help with family relationships rather than moving immediately to placement as a solution.

It is well known that children often become scapegoats for marital problems, and the marriage does not improve simply because the child is removed. Laurie's worker may have reacted to her own need to protect Laurie from an upsetting family situation, as the parents were drinking and arguing about her. The solution of removal may seem preferable to the worker, but might not be Laurie's choice: she is probably used to the fighting; she may also feel that she is being blamed and punished by being placed elsewhere.

Sometimes the demands for immediate placement came from caregivers. The child in the following case was in an adoptive home, pending legalization at the end of a six-month trial. The principle is applicable, however, to foster care.

> David, five, had been placed for adoption with the E. family. They were demanding that the agency remove him because of his difficult behavior. The worker said, "I have felt all along that the [adoptive] parents' marital situation is tenuous and that David is scapegoated in order to move attention away from their own marital problems. These parents in fact have never really bonded to David. I can see that being impulsive, guilt-ridden people, they would not want to have an opportunity to work matters out with David. Their solution has always been to get rid of David."

The worker's final comment seems overstated, as the E. family must have wanted David in their home initially; the worker sounds angry and judgmental toward the adoptive parents, probably because she is frustrated with the placement breakdown. The agency and the adoptive parents seem to be moving toward confrontation, and David is likely to be the loser. An adversarial stance between the home and the agency will be a barrier to teamwork that could enable David to make a gradual transition to another home.

The power of caregivers is evident in this last example. It is their home, and they have a right to ask for a child's removal. Caregiver power was also shown in the case of Samantha and Ashley, when the worker was unable to control the foster carer's negative remarks about the girls' family. If workers become angry at caregivers, they must recognize and deal with their anger, or it will inhibit their casework in behalf of the child. In the cases just discussed, the paramount principle of the child's best interests seems to have been lost while the agency struggled with the demands of parents or caregivers.

Understanding Parental Ambivalence. When parents pressure a worker to place into care an adolescent whose behavior is disrupting their family life, it should be remembered that an enduring attachment may underlie their temporary frustration.

> Bruce, 14, was the son of middle-class parents who requested placement because, as the worker said, "At school he was a real behavioral problem and at home had no respect whatsoever for Mom and Dad. He would do what he wanted, when he wanted, and was really successful in manipulating them."

> After Bruce came into care the worker noted, "It's interesting how, when the distance between father and son came, their relationship strengthened. At home it wasn't strong at all. Bruce had no respect for his father, and the father had no time for Bruce. He often said to Bruce, 'You must be retarded.'" After Bruce had spent four months in care, however, the worker reported, "The parents are really on a guilt trip about having had Bruce come into care. It was at their request." Bruce's father denied responsibility for

the original decision to place him in care. "The father says, 'I just feel rotten taking him back to the foster home on the weekend...I can hardly do it. I don't believe in families being separated...this is all new to me. I never did agree to it...it was my wife who signed him over. From the beginning I never agreed to it.'"

The father had shown some sense of responsibility for Bruce just before the admission to care. "What father was saying at that time was, 'I'll move out of the house, I'll separate, and keep Bruce with me and we'll go live in an apartment and I'll get him straightened out. Then we [the family] will move back together.' I just scratched my head. That never happened. He never followed up on that, and the outcome was that Bruce came into care."

The worker gave no explanation for not having pursued the father's earlier offer to take responsibility for Bruce, except to express confusion by "scratching his head." He may have been puzzled about whether to follow up on the father's suggestion, which was unusual and involved leaving the rest of the family. Or he may have thought Bruce would be better away from his father, who was denigrating him. Certainly, the father seemed ambivalent, first rejecting, then offering to care for Bruce; after placement, the positive side of this ambivalence seems to have strengthened.

In a decision about placement based on difficult adolescent behavior, agencies should consider that parents' negative feelings toward their child are probably heightened by frustration and exhaustion in a living situation that seems intolerable to them. With placement, we can expect parents to feel immediate relief; their painful memories begin to fade, and their basic filial attachment gradually surfaces. If agencies have based their decision for placement on signs of parental rejection, they may have overlooked positive feelings that could have provided a basis for keeping the family together. Even when placement is inevitable, it is important that agencies not allow themselves to be railroaded by parents into treating the situation as an emergency and making the placement in a rush, without adequate preparation.

Discussion

Supervisory Help to Workers

Helpful supervisory techniques were illustrated when supervisors reminded workers of basic skills for eliciting children's feelings, and used gentle prompts to support competent practice. These supervisors identified separation issues, asked relevant questions, and made suggestions. They also linked the workers' observations of the children's behavior with psychosocial theory. When the workers were caught between the competing needs of children, parents, and foster carers, these supervisors upheld the principle of priority to child's interests.

Understandably, supervisors could be relatively objective and could help workers gain insight into their own feelings. The supervisors were one step removed from the pain created by separation, consequently they would not have the same need to minimize the importance of children's relationships with their families.

It was a major weakness of supervisors, however, that they often did not follow up their own initiatives. When the workers did not respond to the point they were making, the supervisors tended to allow the topic of separation to lapse. Ideally, they could have discussed specific interventions the worker might use to help a particular child with separation. Such specific discussions are a means by which supervisors can verify whether workers have grasped what the supervisors have said. In effect, how does the worker intend to handle the situation?

Examples of supervisors helping workers with separation issues were found in only six cases, all of which were discussed in this chapter. Furthermore, when workers reported practices that were contrary to accepted theory, supervisors rarely questioned them. Possible reasons for this nonintervention by supervisors include lack of knowledge, personal preference for an exclusive model of foster care, a bureaucratic orientation toward protecting the status quo, and identification with the workers' discomfort.

In terms of knowledge, it was expected that supervisors would have the required training and/or experience to help workers understand separation theory and its practice implications. The supervisors participated in the two-day workshop provided by the project and led their workers in a subsequent half-day workshop to discuss their own cases. It may be that supervisors have no more theoretical knowledge of separation than their workers. In the author's academic experience, most social work education does not include content on separation as part of the core curriculum. Even when supervisors did have theoretical knowledge, they may not have been able to translate this into ideas for intervention that could be passed on to workers.

Some supervisors may hold an orientation of exclusiveness in foster care, like the supervisor who laughed at the mother's angry reaction to Danny calling his foster carer "Mom." Others may accept inclusiveness theoretically, but be unwilling to challenge established agency norms. As discussed earlier, child welfare agencies place high priority on keeping their foster carers satisfied, and foster carers who are used to an exclusive approach may reject involvement with children's families. The author experienced this while training CAS workers apart from this study: a foster care worker expressed dismay that inclusion was being advocated, saying the agency's foster carers were promised, during the process of approval, that they would not have to be involved with families.

Supervisors may also be reluctant to press workers to deal with separation because they identify with workers' discomfort, just as workers back away when they sense children are fearful of talking about their families. The author has experienced this in supervising workers, who often became defensive when faced with the painful prospect of discussing separation with children, and found reasons to avoid or delay doing so. This pattern may explain why some supervisors, when the workers did not respond to supervisor-initiated discussions, did not persist.

Agency Practices and Structures

Agency practices and structures often reflected the low priority given to maintaining children's family ties. Agency support for visits seemed to depend more on the parent-worker relationship than on the children's needs. There was little indication that agencies questioned or tried to influence the behavior of foster carers who excluded parents. Examples of exclusiveness toward children's families included denying their importance, maintaining distance from them, or using parental titles that created confusion and pain for children and their parents, as illustrated in the cases of Angel and Danny. It appeared that the agencies colluded in excluding parents, since there was no evidence that they questioned or corrected the foster carers.

As discussed earlier, agencies are likely to support the interests of foster carers in the cause of preserving their placement resources. This gives power to foster carers. In the author's experience, workers who were inexperienced or did not have strong convictions about inclusiveness could be intimidated by resistance from long-term foster carers. The latter were unaccustomed to inclusive practice and could cite agency tradition for support. Nevertheless, a social worker in a CAS training session, who had been a matron of a children's home in Britain, reported transferring her approach to parents there to her CAS practice in Canada: she assumed foster carers would welcome parents to their homes and she apparently met with no resistance.

It is notable that the only workers who reported implementing the separation training in their practice were those who had minimal exposure to agency norms. Experienced workers may have resisted adopting an inclusive approach because it did not fit with established agency practice.

Conclusions

Generally, there was an absence of leadership by supervisors to move workers toward more sensitive practice. Even with special training, it seems that supervisory leadership to follow accepted theory cannot be taken for granted, and agencies must build in policies and structures if they are to safeguard placement principles. Agency procedures and structures should be oriented toward providing continuity for children, building positive attitudes toward families, establishing agency-foster carer collaboration, and taking a child-centered response to demands for moving children. These points are discussed further as recommendations in Chapter Six.

References

Steinhauer, Paul. (1974). *How to succeed in the business of creating psychopaths without even trying.* Paper presented to Annual Meeting of Ontario Children's Aid Societies, Toronto, ON.

Chapter Six
Conclusions and Recommendations

This study has analyzed the literature on separation and placement research with respect to maintaining family ties for children in foster care. It has added to practice knowledge by exploring placement practices in two urban child welfare agencies, in relation to children's reactions to separation and the treatment of their family relationships by workers and agencies. The overall picture is that children in care have strong emotional ties to their families, but these often go unrecognized, while families tend to be excluded from their children's lives in care. The study's findings are supported by the literature. The conclusions and recommendations below are presented according to their implications for children, families, foster carers, workers, and agencies.

Children

Confirmation of Separation Theory

The pain and confusion experienced by most children in out-of-home care was illustrated in the workers' discussions with their supervisors. The children's feelings were reflected in withdrawn or aggressive behavior, which was likely to affect the success of placements. Thus, child welfare workers must intervene to help children with the separation experience and its lasting effects.

The most helpful form of intervention with children seemed to be support from their families. When children were accompanied by family members to an unfamiliar home, they tended to express their anxiety and sadness directly, rather than through

213

aggressiveness or withdrawal. This gave the children's workers and families a chance to respond to their pain; the children, for their part, showed an increased readiness to accept placement.

Developing Agency Structures
to Provide Continuity for Children

Providing Information to Link Past and Present. The importance of giving background information to children in out-of-home care was reinforced by this study's finding of a pattern of children in long-term care not asking questions about their past until they reached adolescence. Their basic questions seemed to be: Why am I living apart from my family? Was I rejected? How do my parents feel about me now? What is happening to my family in my absence? Workers who helped adolescents to fill these gaps in their knowledge reported beneficial results.

These findings support the contention in the literature that many children lack the information they need to develop a realistic account of the past and a sense of identity. Agencies should standardize the communication of family information to children with the use of such aids as cameras for family photographs, and with institutionalized procedures such as constructing a Life History Grid [Anderson & Brown 1980] or a genogram [Melina 1980] with all children in care. Ideally, lifebooks should be created for all children in care, not just those moving to adoption or long-term placement; family information should be routinely obtained at placement so that these tools can be made meaningful to children.

Children should also be made aware, at an early age, that they have a right to information about their families. Ontario legislation directs agencies to inform children in care about their right to information about themselves. Given their dependency on their workers and foster carers, however, children may be afraid of repercussions if they exercise these rights. Thus, it is important for workers to be proactive and support children in accessing information that will help them to integrate their past and present lives.

Assuring Continuity of Care. Workers and supervisors often minimized the risks to children when they experienced discontinuity in care. When asked to report on their interventions in relation to separation, the workers gave little evidence of having prepared children for moves or having encouraged parents to prepare them. This picture was reinforced by the reports of two graduate students in the author's classroom experience who had worked in different group homes in the late 1980s. They recalled that many CAS workers chose to move adolescents without any warning, rationalizing that the children might be upset and run away if they were forewarned of a move.

The literature review and study findings suggest several ways in which agencies can build in continuity for children in care: choosing a familiar placement, involving a familiar person in a move, preparing children for preplacement visits, and minimizing worker and home changes.

When children cannot stay with their own families, a natural alternative is for them to move in with relatives. The benefits of kinship placements were noted in the literature review, yet they were seldom used by the two CASs studied. Agencies may not want to place children in the homes of relatives because the relatives often have low incomes or their physical facilities may not meet those expected of traditional foster homes. Agencies also may fear that they will lose some control when they place a child with relatives, especially if parents can visit at will, or if there is tension between parents and relatives. Moreover, CASs may be reluctant to pay children's relatives to care for them, fearing that this will set a precedent.* These concerns, however, would seem to be more than offset by the psychological value of the child's sense of belonging to, and identification with, rela-

---

* In Ontario, families caring for the children of relatives can receive a provincial foster care allowance, without any involvement with a child protection agency, but the amount is generally less than a CAS pays to an approved home. When a CAS asks relatives to take a child, the CAS is expected to pay the carers from the agency budget, which ultimately costs taxpayers more.

tives. If we value continuity for children, then kinship homes should be considered as the first placement option.

Separation theory highlights the importance of having children accompanied by familiar persons, preferably parents, when they enter care or move to another home. There were only a few examples, however, of parents being included in a preplacement visit or move into care; in moves from one agency home to another, there was no evidence of involving the child's own parents. Children should not have to move without a familiar person, ideally a parent, coming with them to offer support. Considering the changes in homes and workers experienced by many children, a parent may be the only continually familiar person in their lives.

Only one child was reported as having a preplacement visit to prepare him for a move, although most agencies provide for such visits in their protocols. Workers cite the lack of time and an unwillingness to keep children another night in their own homes as reasons for moving them without a preplacement visit, yet the shock of sudden placement must surely be damaging to a child's psychological well-being.

Some children had to change workers when they were admitted to care, or when they moved to a new home, times of great vulnerability for them. These practices evolve from bureaucratic structures: in some agencies, children entering care are transferred from a family worker to a children's worker, or workers are assigned to foster homes, rather than to children. Thus, children lose a familiar worker at the same time as they lose a familiar home. Some children had to move because their initial placement was treated as an emergency and they could not stay in the first home.

As children in care are already experiencing too many changes in their lives, agency structures that build in additional disruption must be questioned. Children should not be introduced to new workers at a time when they are changing homes, nor should short-term placements be used, except in unavoidable emergencies. Although it may be awkward for agencies to change long-standing practices, priority should be given to children's feelings and well-being over institutional considerations. Organizational structures that require children to undergo additional changes of placement and workers are difficult to justify, even in economic terms. A cost-benefit analysis might show that gains in short-term efficiency are later lost. Children who experience changes early in their placement may be wary of ever allowing themselves to depend on any one home or worker again. The resulting behavioral problems and/or serial placements could well consume more worker time than was saved by bureaucratic structures.

Finally, another type of discontinuity is created for children when other children living with them are moved in and out of their foster placements, inexplicably and without warning. The literature indicates that this creates fear and confusion for all the children in the placement. Children who observe others around them being moved with little warning or explanation, and have had similar experiences themselves, have reason to live in fear that more changes are coming. To prevent this, either workers or foster carers should prepare the children for impending changes affecting other children, as much in advance as possible. It is natural for children to be apprehensive when they are warned about an upcoming move; they may even act out their feelings. Nevertheless, this opportunity to react gives the children added control over the situation. It is better for their mental health to express resistance about an upcoming change, than to carry around free-floating anxiety in expectation of imminent change and loss.

Families

The theory, literature, and empirical findings have all highlighted the potential damage to children of separation from their families. More effort is needed to prevent separation through programs to support families and the use of modified placement models. When prevention is not feasible, workers should be committed to inclusive placement practice.

Family Support

Creative programs to support families have been expanding in recent years, with the recognition of the struggles faced by many families: economic hardship, lone parenting, and adolescent unpreparedness for the parent role. These programs usually began in family service and mental health agencies, and have recently been offered by some child protection agencies with the goal of preventing placement. Family support rests on the principles of the importance of reaching out to families before they break down, the value of informal/natural supports, and the right of families to parenting education, primary health care, high-quality child care, early childhood education, parent support/self-help centers, information and referral, income support, and housing. Ideally, family support programs are broadly targeted to build parental competence in aspects of their lives beyond child care—jobs, school, interpersonal relationships—in the belief that this competence will enhance parental functioning. Under the umbrella of family support, a broad range of services is offered: in-home aides (homemakers/parent aides), day care, respite care, family-centered casework, and intensive family-centered crisis services.

The programs most relevant to the families in this study are family-centered casework (FC) and intensive family-centered crisis (IFC) services. FC services aim to help families stay together or, failing this, to work toward the return to families of their children in care. The methods used include counselling, education/skill building, advocacy, provision of concrete services, and helping families strengthen their support networks. FC services provide help with a range of family problems, such as inadequate resources for physical survival, violence, neglect, substance abuse, child-parent conflict regarding behavior, parent out of home (in mental health or correctional facilities), problems related to adolescent parenting, and children in out-of-home care. Of particular relevance to this study, they provide services with respect to parent-child visiting and family reunification.

IFC services, which incorporate Homebuilder-type programs and family preservation services, are more intensive and crisis-oriented than FC services. They target families in serious crisis, with the goal of protecting children, strengthening families, preventing out-of-home placement, or helping families through the critical period when their children first return from foster care. They are based in the theory and practice of crisis intervention, viewing a family crisis as upsetting the homeostasis and providing an opportunity for constructive change, with timely and appropriate help. The methods of IFC services are similar to but more intensive than those of FC services: help tends to be given in the home, often involving parent-aides who supplement parental care and model child care and handling of parent-child conflict.

The main limitation of the above programs is that they are not consistently available across the child welfare system; many are time-limited demonstration projects. Established programs are usually based on a short-term model, in which services are withdrawn after the crisis passes. Families that are weakened by structural disadvantage often require intensive, long-term support: they have inadequate resources as well as marginal status in their communities. Child welfare agencies should ensure that FC and IFC programs are available to prevent placement and help parents to reunite with children from whom they have been separated.

An excellent long-term support model is provided by the Community Family Treatment Program at Chedoke-McMaster Child and Family Centre (Hamilton, Ontario). It is similar to Homebuilder-type programs, but recognizes that some families need extended service. This recognition comes from its history as a foster care treatment program in which foster carers (called "parent therapists") were encouraged to work with children's own families [Levin et al. 1976]. In its present family treatment program, "long-term" families may have a parent therapist in their homes up to several days per week, with 24-hour telephone access for crises, for several years if necessary. This flexibility is realistic with families whose parenting problems are complicated by structural disadvantage, as their needs do not lessen appreciably with short-term or occasional intervention.

Although most professionals would agree that some families are so overwhelmed that they need long-term support, agencies may be reluctant to provide this because of the cost. Such programs, however, are less expensive than caring for the troubled children who enter care if their families do not receive the support they need. In addition to the high per diem cost of group care, agencies often provide a one-on-one worker for disturbed youths. The families of these youths might be able to cope with them at home, however, with support from a parent therapist or a one-on-one youth worker. Presumably the youths would be less disturbed if they were spared the confusion and feelings of rejection that are likely to accompany separation. A well-resourced in-home support program provides an opportunity to strengthen family bonds, so that parents may begin to meet their children's need for "someone who really cares." The results of this study suggest that behaviorally disturbed youths are unlikely to have this need met by a substitute caregiver, because their placements with such carers tend to be unstable.

Modified Care

When preventive efforts are insufficient, and children must enter care, the literature and this study have revealed a high risk of families withdrawing from contact with their children. Modified forms of out-of-home care can provide supplemental care to children and relief to parents, while preserving family relationships. As mentioned in the literature review, such models include foster day care [Pavelson 1972], short-term placement with neighbors [Barr 1971], placement on weekends only [Astrachan & Harris 1983], placement during the week and return home on weekends [Balbernie 1974; Loewe & Hanrahan 1975], and periodic short-term placement to help parents through critical periods [Gabinet 1983].

Although rarely used, modified arrangements support families by filling some of the gaps in their parenting, while affirming the importance of family ties. They are consistent with the options open to middle- and high-income families, who may also have difficulty in their parenting role, either chronically or in stressful periods. These families have the resources to hire nannies or send their children to boarding school or camp at those times when the family's emotional resources are drained, or the children need more structure in their lives. Low-income parents should not have to forfeit their rights to their children because they cannot pay for substitute care.

The main barrier to modified care is probably the tendency for workers, when confronted with a crisis, to turn to traditional responses. Workers are familiar and comfortable with the typical model of foster care in which one family carries the total parenting role, and may be reluctant to try a new approach. Workers may also be afraid of criticism from the community if children who have been neglected are still living at home part-time. Consequently, the use of modified care needs to be explored and sanctioned at the agency level. It requires flexibility and adaptation from foster carers and workers, but gives a clear message to parents that the agency supports them in continuing to take responsibility for their children.

Helping Families Remain Involved

The evidence in this study suggests that it is difficult to keep parents involved in traditional full-time placements. Agencies can create a climate that encourages families to stay involved with their children by adopting inclusive practices: involving families in a move from the beginning, conveying positive attitudes regarding families to foster carers, and facilitating regular contact.

Including Families in Placements from the Beginning. As indicated above, most children were moved without parental accompaniment. Besides depriving children of support, this communicates to parents that they are not viewed as important to their children. Agencies should institutionalize an inclusive orientation to care by including it in their initial orientation of foster carers. They should introduce children's parents to their foster carers as early as possible in the placement process, ideally at a preplacement visit. A personal meeting allows people to experience each other as human beings. If foster carers only hear about the parents in terms of their failure to care for their children, and biological parents view the foster carers primarily as competitors for their children's allegiance, they will have difficulty accepting each other. Empirical evidence links positive attitudes on the part of foster carers' with frequent parental visiting: the association is especially strong with visiting by mothers but is also significant with visiting by fathers [Palmer 1983]. It may be expected that parents and foster parents will be more likely to work together in behalf of children if the social worker facilitates a relationship between them at the beginning of the placement. If this is not an agency norm, it should be encouraged by supervisors and by in-service training.

Eliciting Positive Attitudes from Foster Carers. In the case examples, some foster carers demonstrated an exclusive attitude toward children's families, and a few were openly negative about them. Only occasionally did workers try to change these attitudes; some workers may have contributed to foster carers' negativity by apparently condoning it, as in the case of Danny. It is important for agencies to focus on parents' strengths, in the interest of protecting children's self-esteem: children draw heavily on their families in forming their own self-concepts. This is especially important for children who have no family contact: if their only information comes through foster carers and workers, who appear to be discounting their parents or labeling them as bad, the children are unlikely to feel good about themselves.

In orientation and ongoing work with foster carers, agencies should take the view that children's family ties are natural and desirable, based on theories of attachment and self-concept formation. Discussions about child-parent ties should begin at the time of placement, so that children feel it is acceptable to talk about their families. Furthermore, caregivers should be discouraged from using parental titles, to avoid confusion for children. The simplest solution is to use first names. If some older foster carers find this objectionable, they can substitute a more neutral title such as "Aunt" or a special nickname.

Involving foster carers and parents may create some discomfort or conflict for them and the workers, but it is preferable to the usual pattern of segregating the two families, which leaves children to deal internally with the conflict.

Encouraging Regular Family-Child Contact. Some children in the study had minimal or no contact with their parents; in a few cases, agencies seemed to discourage visits. Other research has revealed influences that work against family-child contact [Proch & Hess 1987]: first, agencies often react to children's distress around visiting by reducing contact; second, parents who are not given a regular visiting schedule are unlikely to visit. Parents may not take the initiative regarding access to their children because they are intimidated by the agency, especially if they have lost in an adversarial court hearing. With so many influences preventing or impeding visiting, agencies should have definite policies encouraging contact. Yet a survey of agencies regarding parental visiting revealed a lack of specific standards for frequency and location of visits [Proch & Hess 1987].

Office-supervised visits should only be used in unusual

circumstances, for example, with parents who are potentially dangerous to their children or who continually abuse the arrangement of coming to the foster home. Ideally, parents should be welcome in the home where their children are living; a friendly atmosphere allows children to relate positively to two sets of caregivers without feeling disloyal to either. In this respect, children in care are similar to children whose parents have separated; the latter have been found to adjust better when their parents are able to cooperate in planning for the children's care [Wallerstein & Blakeslee 1989].

The principle of welcoming parents into the foster home is exemplified by an experimental program called Family Partners, developed by one of the CASs taking part in this study [Fong 1994]. This program views biological parents and foster carers as forming a holistic union, like an extended family, for the purpose of caring for the child. The foster carers encourage biological parents to visit in their home and assume a teaching role with them; they sometimes provide support with other problems in their lives, such as substance addiction, that are crucial to the reunion of the family. The experiment included 20 foster homes over a four-year period, and was successful enough that the model is being introduced into the agency's regular foster home program.

Groups for Parents. A creative way to support parents' involvement with their children is to encourage them to join with others who are sharing similar experiences. Ideally, agencies should organize self-help groups for the parents of children in care, as some agencies have done [Levin 1992]. These groups give families a chance to share their experiences: it can be comforting to parents to know they are not alone, and can bolster their self-esteem to see that others have also struggled in their parenting roles. Group members can support each other in continuing to take responsibility for their children; they are likely to gain strength by hearing from each other that they are important to their children.

In summary, many children and adolescents presently entering foster care might be served appropriately by alternatives such as family treatment or modified forms of placement. It is important that staffing and funding patterns be flexible enough to offer families the least intrusive service that will help them through a critical time. For families whose children are fully separated from them, there must be encouragement, from foster carers and workers, for continued involvement in their children's lives.

Foster Carers

Discontinuity in Placements

Probably the most troubling aspect of foster care revealed by the study is its discontinuity. Many children had to be moved at least once, which represented further rejection for them. Moreover, the greatest risk of disruption concerns children who are already disturbed and who have experienced multiple rejections. The findings suggest that a possible cause of placement breakdown may be the foster carers' expectation that children will become part of their families and the children's difficulty in making these attachments. This lack of fit leads to disappointment for foster carers, while children experience confusion and a sense of failure.

The disruptive effect on children who have to move is compounded when foster carers press workers to move them quickly. Andy, for example, was moved by his foster carer without a preplacement visit; his worker was ill but there was no mention of waiting until she came back. The worker's discussion indicated that this was normal practice. The author's experience supports this general impression. Typically, foster carers would not report difficulties with a child until the foster carers were at the breaking point and wanted an immediate move. Workers had trouble slowing such moves down so they could adequately prepare the child for a new home. Generally, children in care could expect to be moved, and they would probably be moved quickly, in response to an exasperated caregiver.

Are Foster Carers Volunteers or Team Members?

Foster carers may be drawn to exclusive practices because of the inadequate compensation they receive from agencies. The pay received by regular foster carers is considered to be compensation for their expenses, but ignores the time and work involved in caring for someone else's children. In this sense, foster carers are treated as volunteers. In the absence of adequate pay, it is understandable that foster carers may expect to be compensated in kind, that is, by having children join their families. When children do not respond to these expectations, the caregiver's commitment may well diminish.

Treating foster carers as volunteers builds into the problem of children having to be moved in haste. Although workers may need time to find a suitable home and take the child on a preplacement visit, they rarely have this opportunity. Because regular foster carers are paid only for their expenses, not their work, agencies tend to defer to their wishes about whether and when a child will leave. Carers are not treated as professionals, so it is expected that they will give priority to their own needs, and workers are disinclined to press them to make further sacrifices of themselves and their families.

Treatment Foster Care and Its Principles

A possible solution for the problems of multiple placements and hurried moves from one placement to another is treatment foster care, which is geared to children and adolescents who have not done well in previous placements. Treatment foster carers are given more training, support, recognition, and pay than regular foster carers and have shown themselves able to handle very damaged children and adolescents in their own homes. Treatment foster care costs more than traditional family foster care, but less than residential treatment. If children who are disturbed are allowed to experience repeated rejection, society eventually pays a high price: many inmates of our jails and psychiatric hospitals have a history of being shunted from one placement to another.

Some of the methods developed in treatment foster care could be adapted for use in regular foster care. Generally, foster carers should be treated as paraprofessionals: agencies should compensate them adequately, provide them with ongoing training and support, share information with them, and expect them to work with children's families.

Foster carers should be compensated at a level that recognizes their personal sacrifice and emotional commitment. With this recognition, they would be less likely to expect children's loyalty, or to try to exclude parents from their lives. As team members, paraprofessional foster carers are likely to alert workers earlier when they are feeling overwhelmed by difficulties with a child, so they can be given support. They are likely to tolerate difficult children longer than regular carers; when they do request a move, they can be expected to cope until the agency finds a suitable home and goes through preplacement preparation with the child.

Ongoing training for foster carers is another aspect of treatment foster care. Training in separation theory, for example, will help carers understand why children may be withdrawn or aggressive, so that they do not interpret this as their own failure, or feel rejected. With a clear understanding of separation, foster carers will be ready to cooperate with drawn-out moves, so that children may be fully prepared. Another form of support can be given by organizing groups of foster carers to act as extended families, meeting to share their concerns and taking turns relieving each other of child care.

Treating foster carers as paraprofessionals also means sharing information freely with them, and encouraging open communication with parents. The latter can begin with parents accompanying their children on a preplacement visit; the parents can inform caregivers about the child's routines, habits, and prefer-ences. This would also respond to the common complaint by foster carers that they receive too little information from workers about children placed in their homes. Building on the initial sharing, workers could encourage ongoing communication between parents and caregivers throughout the placement. Encouraging foster carers to work with parents improves the chances of a positive relationship between the two families, which reduces internal conflict for children. It also allows foster carers to move from the ambiguous role of trying to replace parents to being paraprofessionals who are supporting the total family unit. Having a clear role is likely to bring carers increased job satisfaction. It may also allow them to continue seeing children after those children are reunited with their families. As mentioned in the study, foster carers often have a sense of loss when they have nurtured children who are then moved. Developing a relationship with the whole family during placement would allow carers to be in touch with the family and to offer the family continuing support.

It is easier for agencies to include foster carers in case planning when their role is that of paraprofessionals. Agencies can feel increased comfort about sharing confidential information, and with having foster carers and parents sit down at the same table. As the two sets of caregivers are already expected to work together, workers spend less time and energy dealing with tensions between them and more time working out a mutually acceptable plan for the child. On the child's part, knowing that both sets of caregivers are working together is reassuring and precludes divided loyalties.

Including Families Works

Finally, the results obtained by a few workers who implemented the training provided by this project show that an inclusive approach to foster care is feasible. Some workers doubted that foster carers would accept parents coming to their homes, or that

theory and research suggest that children will be more upset if their questions are not answered. Those who do not know their past will tend to imagine the worst, including blaming themselves for the separation.

The training provided by the project encompassed most of the above gaps between theory and practice by advocating a broadly inclusive approach to placement. Although few of the workers reported explicitly using the training, when the 36 trained workers were compared one year later with controls who received no training, the trained workers had reunited more families. This suggests that the trained workers may have become more aware of the damaging effects of separation and tried harder to reunite families than the controls. Moreover, the trained workers, when faced with a decision to reunite children or keep them in care, may have been more favorably disposed toward reunion than were the controls. The apparent effectiveness of the project training with new workers suggests that agencies should provide training in separation issues to all their workers as part of orientation. This would help to prevent workers from following agency placement practices that ignore recognized theory and principles. The project also demonstrated that an inclusive approach was feasible and had the desired results for the few workers who did implement it.

In summary, the study revealed that certain basic principles of child welfare were not reflected in practice. Workers tended to function as good bureaucrats, supporting the interests of foster carers who were a valuable agency resource, and being cautious about giving information to clients. Unfortunately, these functions detracted from their role as social workers, in which they are expected to give priority to client needs and share relevant information with them. Generally, workers did not respond sensitively to the needs of children being separated from their families. Training in separation appeared to be helpful, especially if given early in a worker's career.

Workers' Response When Parents Demand Immediate Placement of Their Children into Care

Reasons for Acceding to Parents' Demands. When workers were pressed by parents to place their children, usually adolescents, they tended to acquiesce. Not only did they place the children, but they tended to treat the placements as emergencies (no preplacement visits and no parental accompaniment).

Why did the workers react so quickly to parental demands? They may have been overwhelmed by too much work: most child protection workers seem to be overburdened, and overworked staff members commonly protect themselves from aggravating demands. One way for staff members to do this is to meet the needs of the parties with the most power, in this case the parents, even at the expense of others, in this case the children. Another reason for acceding to parents' requests might be the workers' instinct to protect children whom they viewed as being rejected by their families. Yet placement is not a solution for rejection; children who are placed at parental request are likely to view this as the ultimate rejection.

Pitfalls of Acceding to Parents' Demands. A decided disadvantage of allowing parents to dictate the terms of an adolescent's placement is that it is difficult for workers to regain control. In the author's experience, adolescents who are "rescued" from rejecting families by CASs often move themselves back home unilaterally soon after placement. Moreover, parents who successfully request placement because of conflicts with their children may vacillate and allow the adolescents to return home without waiting for agency approval. In effect, the placement changes the internal balance of the family. When parents are relieved of a major source of stress, they may begin to feel guilty about the placement or jealous of the new caregivers. If they have been able to control the terms of placement, they are likely to allow the adolescent to return without ever dealing with the problems that led them to request placement.

Responding Effectively to Parents' Request for Help. The agency hierarchy can be used to help workers respond effectively to parents' demands for placement: to make a good decision, to contract with the family for ongoing work, and to involve the family with placement. Supervisors can be more objective than workers in making decisions because they are not exposed to direct pressure from parents. As for ongoing work with the family, agencies have the greatest leverage with parents before the decision is made, when they still have the power to grant or refuse the request for placement. It is important for workers to challenge parental assumptions that all their problems will be solved by placement. Workers should engage the parents in examining how the whole family may have contributed to the crisis and how they may work during placement toward future reintegration.

A final condition for granting the parents' request should be their agreement to participate in the placement process. This includes explaining placement as positively as possible to their children or adolescents, supporting and accompanying them through admission to care, and maintaining regular contact. In all these ways, agencies can provide leadership to workers as they guide families through decision-making, family counseling, and eventual reunion.

Agencies

Discrepancies between principles and practice, to the degree found in this study, must be confronted at an agency level. In discussions prior to the project, senior staff members in both CASs assured the author that their agencies were committed to inclusive practice, yet the evidence from workers reflects a prevailing norm of exclusive practice. Furthermore, both agencies had written protocols prescribing preplacement visits, except for emergencies, yet only one child was given a preplacement visit. As a psychiatrist working with foster carers commented, "It is regrettable that so much thoughtless trauma occurs as a result of psychobiologically unrealistic foster care policies and practices" [Fine 1989].

Reasons for Gap between Principles and Practice

In discussions during training sessions, workers cited lack of time and concerns about parental behavior if parents were taken to the foster home. The importance of preparation and parental presence was supported by the finding that children entering care with these conditions are less likely to be moved again than those who lack such supports. Regarding the attitudes of parents, most of them had requested or accepted placement, so they could be expected to cooperate.

Bureaucratic organizations, like their workers, will tend to make choices that simplify their work. Superficially, it seems easier to hand over total care for a child to one family than to guide the sharing of responsibility between foster carers and parents, especially when there may be distrust between them.

Another obstacle to inclusive practice is the difficulty organizations have in individualizing their responses to clients. Agencies tend to drift into routinized approaches in which they set similar expectations for all parents, such as regular weekly visiting. When parents did not meet these expectations, workers and foster carers commonly became frustrated, as illustrated by their negative or patronizing remarks about parents in the supervisory sessions. It could be assumed that these negative attitudes toward parents were present agencywide, because supervisors hearing negative comments tended to let them slide by.

Supporting Inclusion of Families

Agencies seem to adopt an all-or-nothing view of parental involvement with children: if parents cannot care for their children at home, the agency takes over and excludes them. This seems to be a punitive approach—families who cannot do the whole job have most of their parental rights removed. We should view foster care as an integral part of the continuum of support offered to families, rather than a substitute for parents who have failed.

To counteract the organizational tendency to exclude families, agencies must develop inclusive policies and procedures and make them explicit to workers and clients. The policies should be agencywide, including not just family and children's workers, but placement resource workers and foster carers. Parents should be encouraged to take as much responsibility as they are willing and able to assume, for example, participating in activities such as school visits, haircuts, and decisions about items to be purchased. Ideally, agency expectations should be individualized to suit parents' unique needs and capabilities. If parents agree to assume responsibilities but fail to follow through, agencies that want to work with them can lower the expectations to an attainable level. For example, if parents are unreliable about visits, the expectation might be initially lowered to having them telephone their child if they are going to miss a visit. When parents show an ability to meet minimal expectations, the expectations can be gradually increased.

There may well be some parents who are unwilling to be involved with their children; they will agree to plans but not carry them out. Workers tend to give up on parents, however, without really trying to individualize their expectations. The flexible approach requires patience and agencies should support workers in accepting parents' limitations and reinforcing small gains.

Maximizing Continuity for Children

Some agency structures, such as emergency or assessment homes, and task specializations, create extra moves and changes of workers for children in care. The existing structures are valued by agencies for their administrative efficiency and simplification of workers' roles, but the disruption to children's lives is too high a price to pay. Even in economic terms, a cost-benefit analysis might show that every placement change increases a child's vulnerability to further placement breakdown. The crises that usually lead up to a move and the ensuing confusion make heavy demands on staff time, and may result in the loss of foster carers.

A recommendation for agencies to change their structures, to provide additional continuity for children, is likely to be resisted by those staff members who are comfortable with the status quo. In the author's discussions with workers during training sessions, they usually defended existing systems, and minimized the need to be concerned about the effects on children. Possible reasons why workers may overlook children's needs have been discussed above; in particular, workers who feel overwhelmed cannot be expected to willingly give up a structure that makes their work more manageable in the short term. Consequently, the impetus for change may have to come from supervisors and administrators: they have a better overview of the effects on children, as well as the requisite power to introduce change. During the study, one of the two agencies was considering a change to generic caseloads: this would mean that children would continue to have the same workers as their families, rather than losing contact with their family's worker when they left home.

Conclusion

Some of these recommendations would require radical changes in agencies' service structures and practices, but the findings of this study indicate that radical changes are necessary if children and families are to be truly helped and their reunion facilitated. Agencies must provide leadership to their workers and foster carers if inclusive practice is to be a reality.

References

Astrachan, M., & Harris, D.M. (1983). Weekend only: An alternate model in residential treatment centers. *Child Welfare, 62,* 253–261.

Balbernie, R. (1974). Unintegration, integration and level of ego functioning as the determinants of planned "cover therapy," of unit task, and of placement. *Association of Workers for Maladjusted Children Journal, 2*, 6-46.

Barr, D.H. (1971). "Doing prevention" in Regent Park. *Journal of Ontario Association of Children's Aid Societies, 14*, 8–13.

Fine, P. (1989). *The emotional functioning of children in the foster care system*. Creigton-Nebraska Department of Psychiatry. Unpublished paper.

Fong, H. (1994, May). Social Worker, Resource Unit, Catholic Children's Aid Society of Metropolitan Toronto. Personal communication.

Gabinet, L. (1983). Shared parenting: A new paradigm for the treatment of child abuse. *Child Abuse and Neglect, 7*, 403-411.

Levin, A.E. (1992). Groupwork with parents in the family foster care system: A powerful method of engagement. *Child Welfare, 71*, 457–473.

Loewe, B., & Hanrahan, T.E. (1975). Day foster care. *Child Welfare, 54*, 7–18.

Palmer, S.E. (1983). *The effects of training on CAS workers' handling of separation* (doctoral thesis, University of Toronto).

Pavelson, M. (1972) Foster daycare: An alternative to admission. *Journal of Ontario Association of Children's Aid Societies, 15*, 1-4.

Proch, K., & Hess, P.M. (1987). Parent-child visiting policies of voluntary agencies. *Children and Youth Services Review, 9*, 17–28.

Wallerstein, J., & Blakeslee, S. (1989). *Second chances: Men, women and children a decade after divorce*. New York: Ticknor and Fields.

Appendix A
Two-Day Workshop on Separation

First Day

9:00–9:15   Workers complete questionnaires on their knowledge and attitudes about separation, while Research Coordinator (S. Palmer) discusses with supervisors their responsibilities for miniworkshops and following-up questionnaire completion with workers.

9:15–10:00   Introduction of trainer (Dr. J. Wilkes) by senior staff person. Discussion of training needs, as perceived by workers and supervisors; presentation of course outline, with ideas for incorporating training needs mentioned in above discussion.

10:15–Noon   Separation Theory (Appendix B).
- (a) Separation anxiety (Bowlby).
- (b) Separation as an interruption to normal development of autonomy from parents (Erikson).
- (c) Adaptation to separation (Freud).

1:00–3:00
- (a) Making Separation a Therapeutic Option: Roleplay to demonstrate handling of separation, introduced by Dr. Wilkes.
- (b) Discussion of feelings aroused by roleplay in those who took part.
- (c) Discussion of feelings about roleplay by other participants in training session.

3:15–4:00   Children's Responses to Separation at Different Ages.

4:00–4:30   Discussion by Participants.

Second Day

9:00–9:15   Discussion by Participants: Reactions to previous day.

9:15–10:00 Helping the Very Young Child with Separation. As preparation, workers will have been given an excerpt of an article to read the previous night [F.M. Pile, "Helping the Baby to Move into the Adoption Home," in *The Role of the Baby in the Placement Process* (Philadelphia, PA: Pennsylvania School of Social Work, 1946), pp. 81–86].

10:15–Noon Workers' Own Feelings about Taking Part in Family Separation
(a) Separation can be a positive step for children.
(b) Denial of feelings by workers and children.

1:00–2:30   Roleplay: Participants carry out roleplay on model demonstrated the previous day, in groups of 4-5.

2:45–3:30   Roleplay Report: Report back on roleplay, one group at a time, with each participant reporting how he/she felt during the various scenes.

3:30–4:15   General Discussion on Separation.

4:15–4:30   Evaluation: Participants complete questionnaires evaluating workshop.

Appendix B
Separation Theory Presented to Children's Aid Society Workshop*

A. Introduction

1. Deprivation may be caused by separation, insufficiency of interaction, or distortion.
2. It is difficult to distinguish the actual effect of each variable.
3. The impact of separation experiences will depend on distortion, both prior to and during separation.

B. Research Problems & Controversy on Parental Deprivation

1. Multiple Mothers: Generally thought to have negative effect, but difficult to separate the circumstances leading to this from the effects.
2. Variability in Degree of Damage
   (a) Not all damage is sufficiently gross to be obvious; often appreciable damage can only be detected at more refined levels of observation, i.e., quantitative tests.
   (b) Vulnerability of children differs according to genetic constitution, environmental influence.
3. Specific vs. General Effects
   (a) Depends on what aspect of child is studied; can affect intelligence, language ability, habits (e.g., thumb sucking)

---

* By Dr. James Wilkes

(b) Workers sometimes conclude that, because deprivation has not affected a particular process being studied (e.g., child's school progress), no damage has been done to other processes; it is unjustified to assume that deprivation affects all processes in equal degrees.

4. Diversity in the Nature of Adverse Effects
Depending on basic personalities, some children seem to become "affectionless" while others may cling to parent figures.

5. Permanence of Effect
(a) Even a severely damaged child may improve to some extent if deprivation is relieved.
(b) Impairment to some processes seems more resistant to reversal than impairment of other processes.
(c) Some damages are more obvious and easily observable than others.
(d) Some types of damage are more resistant to reversal.
(e) Some lasting effects are manifested overtly under special circumstances, e.g., more in later life.

6. Association with Delinquency
Bowlby's theories showing that early deprivation experiences will result in children with "affectionless" characters are not always supported by empirical findings.

7. Maternal vs. Environmental Deprivation
Major issue is child's level of stimulation, but people tend to ascribe mystical properties to care given to child by biological mother.

8. Summary
(a) Erroneous to think that a single complex of experiences, more or less prolonged, occurring in early childhood will have a uniform and lasting effect in all cases.
(b) Development of the individual organism is an unbroken process, thus a deprivation experience acts through its influence upon ongoing processes and is interpreted in the light of previous experience.

(c) The ongoing processes on which deprivation acts are, in turn, a result of the whole previous history of development that has taken place through the interaction of the organism with environmental influences.

(d) The response to relief from deprivation is determined both by processes set up in the course of the deprivation experience and by the extent to which they are reinforced, modified or reversed by later organism-environment interaction.

C. Effects of Separation

1. Importance of Attachment

(a) Children cannot really separate if they have not formed a basic attachment, i.e., the effect of separation depends on the nature of the relationship.

(b) Children who have experienced repeated separations usually have damaged capacity to form attachments; to repair this capacity, attention has to be given to earlier separations from parents to whom they were attached.

(c) Bonding is a process of developing attraction and intensity of relationship; bonding is not a permanently fixed relationship but one that develops.

(d) Important factors in the development of bonding are: proximity, frequency and duration of proximity, and behavioral interaction.

(e) Erikson speaks of the development of a child in terms of a cog wheel: there are two wheels (child and environment), each influencing the other.

(f) In mother-infant bonding, "It is as though the baby is making love to the mother before she falls in love with her baby" [Crowcroft, in *Canadian Psychiatric Association Journal*, 25(5) (August 1980)].

(g) John Bowlby, using an ethnological model for his statements on attachment, speaks of attachment being recognized by maintaining proximity, feeding, or aggressive behavior toward an errant partner or those who would attempt to separate one from the object of attachment.

2. Separation from Biological Parents Is Never Complete
   (a) Separation may be permanent in the sense that geographically the individuals may never again be in physical proximity, but it is never complete, because it lives in history and memory. Even where there has been separation at birth, the biological parents live in the child's fantasy.
   (b) Because separation can never be complete, workers must not seek to erase attachments to parents before moving on to make plans for children who require permanent out-of-home placement.

3. Dynamics of Separation
   (a) Intervening variables include ego strength, past experience, and present circumstances.
   (b) Circumstances include age, degree of disruption and distortion, degree of deception, and nature of previous parenting/attachment.
   (c) The mourning process encompasses:
       (i) protest, shown by irritability and anger;
       (ii) despair, shown by withdrawal and apparent depression; and
       (iv) resolution, shown by child being apparently "back to normal," or seeming detached.

4. Consequences of Separation Dependent on Many Variables
   (a) Number and duration of previous separations.
   (b) Success of the establishment of substitute attachments.
   (c) Quality and nature of primary parental relationship: consistency, stability, and rationality.
   (d) Extent to which child has achieved healthy developmental milestones.

(e) Presence or absence of deviant or regressive personality characteristics in the child.

(f) Balance in use of defense mechanisms: adaptive or maladaptive.

(g) Presence and degree of developmental handicaps, e.g., physical illness, physical deformity, developmental delays.

(h) Family constellation and birth order, and presence of siblings in home or in placement.

(i) Extent to which parent or parents are or were able to prepare child for this experience.

(j) Extent to which the receiving placement is able to meet child's needs and recognize child's individuality, including cultural and environmental fit.

(k) Behavioral symptoms displayed.

5. Making Separation a Therapeutic Option

(a) Know one's own feelings.

(b) Tell the truth.

(c) Avoid editorializing, e.g., "There is a need for this," "We do our best," "Don't be upset," "Try hard to behave."

Appendix C
Guidelines for
Separation Workshop Roleplay

Roleplay:
Making Separation a Therapeutic Option

Participants: Dr. Wilkes, as social worker.
Caroline Chiaisson, as foster carer.
Sharon Hinton, as three-year-old being placed.
Biological parents and male foster carer (played
by volunteers from participants in training).

Scene 1: In Family Home Prior to Admission

Participants: Social worker, biological parents, child.
Purpose: Discussion of apprehension of child.
Situation: Parents have left Sharon alone after being warned
last time they did this that continued lack of
supervision would result in admission to care.
Duty worker was called at midnight previous
night, decision was made to have a homemaker
(retained by agency) stay with Sharon overnight.
Worker comes to home in morning, by which
time parents have returned.

General Points to be Covered:

1. Social worker discusses reasons for apprehension with parents, then has them tell Sharon that she is going to a foster home and why.

2. Parents express feelings to Sharon about what has happened (e.g., they are sorry, or they are angry at agency).

3. Parents tell Sharon what to expect re visits from them and possible return home.

Scene 2: At Foster Home

Participants: Foster carers, biological parents, child, social worker.

Purpose: Preplacement visit.

General Points to be Covered:

1. Reassure Sharon that her biological parents know where she is, and that the foster carers know why she is in care.
2. Reinforce Sharon's trust in her parents, as she will not trust other adults if she learns to distrust parents.

Appendix D
Suggested Guidelines for Miniworkshops

Miniworkshop #1

Topic: Nonverbal Methods of Handling Separation

1. Dr. Paul Steinhauer's videotape, "Charlene," is shown. It describes his play therapy with a five-year-old girl, who was in foster care because her parents were killed in a car accident from which she emerged unhurt (45 minutes).
2. Group discussion of how Dr. Steinhauer's approach could be used with children who have been separated from their parents by admission to care (15 minutes).

Break (optional)

3. Roleplay (in pairs) of five-year-old child in care being interviewed by a new worker.
    (a) Worker provides a paper and pencil and asks child to draw a picture of his/her biological family.
    (b) Worker uses the child's drawing as a basis for discussing his/her feelings about the family (likes and dislikes, wishes, fears) and feelings about being in care (15-20 minutes).
4. Discussion of roleplay and questions (remainder of two-hour session, about 30 minutes).

Miniworkshop #2

This session is a form of group supervision, with each worker presenting a case where he/she has tried to implement the training received in dealing with separation. As background material, points made by participants in Miniworkshop #1 are summarized below, with some suggestions from the researcher (S. Palmer). Ideally, the cases presented by workers should illustrate one or more of these points so that discussion can be generalized to answer some of the questions raised earlier.

Points Made by Participants in Miniworkshop #1 Regarding the Nonverbal Approach and Its Implementation

1. Use of play: This was viewed as a good way to encourage children to express feelings. The child has a sense of control over the interview and may achieve some catharsis of negative feelings.
2. Reflection vs. interpretation: Workers generally thought the best response to the child's feelings, as expressed in play, was to comment on the child's behavior and suggest feelings, but not to move too quickly to interpretation for which the child might not be ready.
3. Revisiting the past: This was seen as a means of helping children relive and resolve feelings of separation and rejection. One example was a child who had been told by parents, prior to admission, that he would be placed in foster care if he were bad. It is important for children to hear from biological parents or from a prior worker that there were reasons for placement apart from their behavior. Some workers were reluctant to draw in former foster carers to help resolve the child's past, even if the child requested this. Dr. Steinhauer advocated revisitation of the past as a therapeutic technique. He described helping a disturbed nine-year-old in care to revisit old foster homes where the process of rejection and repression of feelings had begun. The foster care resources department would have to be involved in revisiting foster carers, if the home were still open. The project director talked to resource workers in both agencies and found them receptive to Steinhauer's ideas, but in practice this represents additional work in communicating within the agency.

4. Giving children excuses for placement: Workers sometimes give children socially acceptable reasons why they cannot live at home, e.g., mother has to work. Workers recognize that these reasons are insufficient and their uneasiness about this is likely to be communicated to the child.

5. Normalization of placement: Children may benefit from knowing they are not the only ones living apart from their parents. Workers suggested it may help a child to meet other children in care (e.g., support groups).

6. Including foster carers: Workers should include foster carers in their efforts to help children with separation. First, the foster carer may be upset that the "honeymoon" period is being disrupted by the worker seeking to keep the child's feelings in the open. Second, the foster parent is needed as an ally to carry on the work, especially as the worker's time is scarce.

7. Unrealistic expectations for attachment: Bonding to the foster carers is unlikely to take place before the child's separation feelings have been faced. Thus, it is pointless to wait until children have "settled" or "bonded" into the foster home before attempting to elicit their feelings about the move.

8. Dealing with workers' own feelings about separation: Personal reactions to separation can be a drain on workers' emotional energy. Steinhauer's comfort with allowing himself to cry in front of Charlene gave permission to workers to do this: it can help to create a caring, accepting atmosphere for the child.

Issues Requiring Further Discussion

1. Adolescents: Older children need a different approach than younger children. This was not really addressed during training. Suggestions: Some adolescents might be willing to draw a picture of their families. Others might have done creative writing for school, which they might share with the worker; or they might be asked to write about their experience of coming into care.

2. Heavy caseloads: Workers said they could not deal with all
    the children on their caseloads at this level, because it was
    too time-consuming.
    Suggestions: As theory indicates that much foster home
    breakdown has its beginning in unresolved separation prob-
    lems, workers will probably spend more time in the long run
    if they ignore separation during the "honeymoon" period.
    Foster carers and biological parents should be enlisted to
    help children with separation feelings from the time of the
    preplacement visit.
3. Lack of skill with nonverbal methods: Some workers felt
    poorly prepared to use nonverbal methods of eliciting
    children's separation feelings. They wondered if they should
    be referring children outside the agency to get help.
    Suggestion: The worker should deal with separation, as the
    person who has access to all involved parties and to back-
    ground information on the child. As most social workers have
    had no formal education on dealing with separation, workers
    with in-service training are as well prepared as anyone to deal
    with separation, under supervision.
4. Complex placement situations: Some workers thought par-
    ticular situations might prevent them from using the ap-
    proaches demonstrated in this training. Workers commented
    that some of their children had been in and out of care many
    times, or they had moved many times with their families. In
    other cases, the length of the separation may be uncertain, as
    parents may show up again at any time, or children may be
    relieved to be out of a home in which they were abused.
    Generally, supervisors encouraged workers not to let these
    conditions prevent them from helping children with their
    feelings, e.g., children who are relieved to be in care also
    have some feelings of being rejected by their families and
    they need to talk about both sides of this ambivalence. One
    worker had never discussed the child's father with her "be-
    cause she had four different fathers."

Suggestion: When workers are uncomfortable with situations that are socially disapproved, such as a sequence of common-law relationships, supervisory help should be sought. Otherwise, an awkward situation may inhibit workers from talking with children about their families.

5. Limited contact with child: Workers were hesitant to begin eliciting a child's feelings if they were going to transfer the child to another worker. This limitation did not impede Dr. Steinhauer: he encouraged Charlene to discuss her feelings even though she would be leaving for her grandparents' home in a few weeks. He communicated to the grandparents through the worker and encouraged them to allow Charlene to continue playing through the accident with the police car he gave her. After a few months, she was able to discard the car and move on.

Summary

Generally, the workers recognized the importance of separation issues to adjustment in foster care. They had doubts, however, about their own abilities, the reaction of foster carers, and the risk of doing an incomplete job because of lack of time. Experience suggests that children will take some initiative in getting answers for themselves, from biological parents and foster carers, as well as workers, if the subject is treated openly from the beginning (before the placement). The greatest risk is that the child's past will become a taboo subject and separation feelings will be repressed.

About the Author

Sally E. Palmer, Ph.D., is Associate Professor, School of Social Work, McMaster University, Hamilton, Ontario, Canada. Dr. Palmer obtained her B.A. at the University of Western Ontario, and her M.S.W. and Ph.D. at the University of Toronto. She has worked in several Ontario Children's Aid Societies, as a frontline worker, supervisor, staff trainer, and researcher. Her interest in maintaining family ties comes primarily from her experiences as a worker. Her agency changed from a specialist model, in which children were transferred to a new worker when they were placed in foster care, to a generalist model, in which a child's family worker continued to carry responsibility for the child in placement. In comparing the two models, she found that the specialist model discouraged foster care workers from including children's families in their lives: the workers' allegiance tended to be with the foster carers and they often did not know the families. Alternatively, the generalist workers tended to facilitate family contact, and children were more likely to talk about their past with a worker who was familiar with their families and their lives prior to placement. In Dr. Palmer's subsequent work as a trainer with workers and foster carers, she noted the persistence of attitudes and practices that excluded families. Consequently, she undertook this study to explore in depth the possible impediments and supports to inclusive practice.